"From the day I first met 'Basketball Bill' I knew in my heart that he was a man who would positively affect my life. As a friend, confidante, and mentor, he has set a gold standard example of a life with integrity and character as its foundation. His book *Nothing but Net* is the culmination of his life experiences and how traditional principles will help you overcome seemingly hopeless and devastating events in our lives. Using basketball terminology, *Nothing but Net* signifies the result of what seemed impossible. From the "Insider's Guide to Integrity" to understanding "Bill's Hard Lessons," this book leads you toward an Integrity-Driven life. I loved the book and will use it as a gut-check measure of my character for the rest of my life. I recommend it to all who struggle with life challenges and all that need hope and inspiration. This book prepares you for your shot in life–a *Nothing but Net* shot."

–Bill Montgomery

Entrepreneur

"Integrity jumps off the pages of this book, touching deep! I cried, I laughed, I jumped for successes, and I understood more clearly values, legacy, wholesomeness."

–Ray Robbins

Entrepreneur/co-founder, Mannatech

"'Basketball Bill' Chaffin first captivated me as an exceptional motivational speaker. His new book *Nothing but Net* blew my socks off! Once you begin reading it, you will not be able to stop. This book will be read and re-read many times over. I am getting multiple copies to give as gifts for all my friends and family."

–Frank Harber, Ph. D.

Apologist and Author

"Reading your book was a joy. I enjoyed every page. It's the type of book one hurries through (because you can't wait to get to the next page and then the next) only to reach the end and want to immediately start over and read it again. Bill's book is all beef and no fat. It's easy to read, concise, jam-packed. It touches the heart (the tears I shed several times are proof). It touches one's funny bone. It's heart-wrenching. It's enlightening, alarming, educational. It's inspiring to one's intellect and one's physical well-being."

–Becky Harber

"Whether in legal court or on a basketball court, playing games with people puts our integrity to the test. Bill Chaffin learned life's hard lessons that all of us would rather learn vicariously. His compelling story illustrates how anyone can compromise their highest standards for temporary relief. As he shares the wisdom that came from his crushing experiences, it requires us to review our own motives and integrity. These hard lessons require us all to ask some hard questions of ourselves. I highly recommend that everyone take a short time to read *Nothing but Net*–you'll be better for it!"

–S. Reed Ashwill, CLU, CFP
President, Borden Hamman Agency, Inc

"I just finished reading Bill's book on integrity–WOW. Great practical insight from someone who lived it. We can all learn from this great read."

–Matthew W. Mclntyre
CEO, Puritan Financial Companies

"I was honored to have been selected to review Bill's new book *Nothing but Net*. Having read it cover to cover, I found it to be deeply inspirational. The trials and tribulations that Bill has experienced are a testament to his strength and stature. To have overcome the adversity that he has faced shows true character. I was inspired by the message and overcome by his passion and resolve. I know this book can be an inspiration for others as well."

–Darrel Fritz
President/CEO, Dreamscape Development Group, Inc.

"This is the most honest and forthright book I have ever read. Basketball Bill's message is clear–don't take the risk of ever losing your foundation of integrity! Without integrity, you have nothing. Anything built on false pretenses will never last. Integrity must be in your blood, your demeanor, your thoughts, your words, and your actions. It cannot be contrived, but it can be lost. The uphill battle to regain one's integrity is long and hard."

–Thomas A. McCall
President and Chief Executive Officer

"*Nothing but Net* is very compelling, captivating, and inspiring. The segment on integrity and character communicates clearly the value of having a "moral compass" that is alive and well. Bill's 'darkest hour' illustrates that he is a survivor and an overcomer, as his good attitude and excellent people skills pulled him through some tough times. Bill Chaffin has a love for life and a love for people that is special. This book will have a powerful influence on all those who read it!"

–Kenneth L. Ramsey
Chairman, Monticello Banking Company,
and Owner of Kenneth Ramsey Insurance

"Intriguing...Emotional...A life journey in faith...Bill Chaffin's book, *Nothing but Net* shows us that in life, no matter what the situation is, faith, character, and integrity go far beyond your financial status, job title, or where home is located. Bill's story is one that will compel you to never give up no matter what situation life brings you. Whether you're young or old, it's a must- read. Bill teaches us integrity is the cornerstone of our lives."

–Butch Johnson
Super Bowl Champion Dallas Cowboys

"Bill Chaffin's book is a classic. No one can read it and not be influenced for good. Bill is a gifted writer who makes his story your story. *Nothing but Net* is a beautiful, living story of defeats and victories."

–Charlie "Tremendous" Jones
Executive Books

"It was a great joy to have 'Basketball Bill' Chaffin on our celebration program on the Daystar Television Network, sharing and shooting hoops. His new book, *Nothing but Net*, gives great insight into the much-needed topic of integrity. This book will be of great value to all who struggle with the moral decay of our society and how we can be the solution."

–Marcus D. Lamb
President/CEO, Daystar Television Network

"I have lived across the street from the Chaffins since 1981. I tell you with a sincere heart that Bill Chaffin is rock solid and authentic. I stood with Bill and his wife, Kay, through the highs and the depths that seemed endless. I can think of no man, woman, or child who would not benefit from reading his wise words and heeding his counsel."

–Barbara Baumgartner

"Bill Chaffin's story and message is a wonderful example of how to face the world and handle adversity. Integrity is the #1 ingredient to living a productive and happy life. If you want to take your life to a higher level, this is the book for you! Bill will show you how and what to do."

–Virgil Slentz
President, Property Enterprise

"Are you willing to spend 2-6 hours to improve yourself and your business? If so, then put *Nothing but Net* on your must-read list. It is a quick read that you will find difficult to put down. Bill bares his soul through his darkest days and shows God's wisdom and truth that led him victoriously through those difficult times."

Tim Whitlock
Branch President, First State Bank of Texas

"'Basketball Bill' Chaffin is a great storyteller. He explains the devastating effect of a runaway ego and an overdose of false pride that can produce unimaginable personal and family disaster. Reading this book will awaken your awareness of how priceless the quality of integrity can be. The book is a must-read for any business leader, family head, or anyone suffering heartache brought on by mistakes made in dealing with people. This book is a 'Soul Cleanser' that explains how you can 'get right with God' and your fellow man for life. It will bring tears."

–Benny B. Ellis, Sr., CLU

"It's this simple: your life is equally proportional to the amount of integrity you live by. As Bill puts it so eloquently with so many of his own life experiences and examples, integrity is forever your riches. However, living without it is a quick rich and quicker die. If every individual would live by the unquestionable, indubitable principles in Bill's book in every area of their lives, we would all find what we search for: the answers to why we exist! Divine intervention lives in the soul's integrity!"

–Judy Moody
Urban Publications

"*Nothing but Net*, by William 'Basketball Bill' Chaffin, is a must-read that demonstrates how ethics and integrity are Bible-based and essential in maintaining meaningful relationships, whether they are with one's spouse, friends, or business associates. Bill captures the true spirit of why adherence to a code of values is critical in any association. *Nothing but Net* illustrates how several outstanding CEO's have been role models of success because of their attitudes and lifelong commitment to integrity. The book is primarily instructive for adults; however, young people can learn from it how success and contentment come from a foundation of personal values.

One cannot help but be touched emotionally by the way 'Basketball Bill' has overcome persecution and professional setbacks because of one weak moment when a bad business decision cost him dearly. He was able to rebuild his life and sustain his integrity throughout several years of struggle. One will not find a better primer on the subject of ethics and integrity than *Nothing but Net*."

–Linus Wright
Former Under Secretary of Education,
U.S. Department of Education

NOTHING BUT NET

NOTHING BUT NET

**LIVING WITH
INTEGRITY IS
YOUR BEST SHOT**

WILLIAM "BASKETBALL BILL" CHAFFIN

with
Greg Webster

Dallas, Texas

Nothing But Net

Living with Integrity is Your Best Shot

For information, please contact:

The P3 Press
16200 North Dallas Parkway, Suite 170
Dallas, Texas 75248
www.thep3press.com
972-381-0009

A New Era in Publishing™

ISBN-13:978-1-933651-32-3
ISBN-10: 1-933651-32-6
LCCN: 2008902138

1 2 3 4 5 6 7 8 9 10

For more information
about William "Basketball Bill" Chaffin
please visit:
www.billchaffin.com

DEDICATION

This book is dedicated to my beautiful, loving, and devoted wife, Kathleen Yvonne Chaffin. Although she is no longer with me in this life, for 35 years before her passing, Kay was my best friend, sweetheart, lover, partner, confidante, companion, and biggest cheerleader. She was also a Proverbs 31 woman. The tenth verse asks, "Who can find a virtuous woman? For her price is far above rubies." This kind of woman has immeasurable value. Kay loved with a tough, unconditional love.

This book tells the story of my darkest hour on planet earth. Yet all the while, Kay stood tall by me when the pressure was the greatest. Her strength and commitment helped our son Chad and daughter Noelle do the same.

I also honor my brother, John Chaffin, who became the glue holding my family together mentally, emotionally, and financially during the very tough times I put them through. John, you're my superhero.

TABLE OF CONTENTS

FOREWORD

Bill Chaffin is my friend. Since he left his position with our company a number of years ago, he has remained in touch and in communication, keeping me up-to-date with his activities and involvements, as well as those of his family. It is a joy to watch him progress in life, and I am personally delighted he has completed writing this book.

Bill has "been there and done that." He's had the birthdays. He's walked the walk. Now he shares with his readers the lessons he's learned—and how he learned them. Not every author is so open and honest about his experiences, particularly the parts of his life that aren't so pretty. But Bill doesn't pull any punches, and he is quick to give the credit—and the glory—to the Person to Whom it belongs.

I believe you will both enjoy and benefit from reading *Nothing but Net: Living with Integrity is Your Best Shot.* It's well-written, interesting, and teaches timeless principles. I don't recall a time in our country's history when Bill Chaffin's message would have been more important or more relevant. I encourage you to read it and apply to your own life the principles that can make an enormous difference—not just in you and your personal and business lives, but in the lives of those around you and into the world.

Zig Ziglar
Author/Motivational Teacher

ACKNOWLEDGMENTS

This book is not the end of anything; it is just the beginning of a new chapter in my life.

To begin with, my deepest gratitude goes to Amanda Brinkman, my wonderful niece, who was my all–star word processor.

Thanks goes to Virgil Slentz, one of my two mentors, for being such a good sounding board and confidante.

To Greg Webster, for pulling the book together as my incredible co-writer. Greg, you captured my heart, my pulse and my sports mentality – many thanks.

To the memory of my wife, Kay, for the fundamental core values she passed on to me.

To Kenneth Ramsey, for his encouragement and moral support to launch the writing of my book in the first place.

To my daughter Noelle, for her prayer support and inspiration to stay the course and finish what I started.

To Dr. Frank Harber, my pastor and treasured friend for looking over my shoulder and giving me guidance and also introducing my co-writer to me.

To Russell Lake, graphics artist extraordinaire, for delivering a unique dust jacket and for doing the layout of my book.

To Zig Ziglar, for his long standing friendship and vote of confidence.

To Laurie Magers, for her wisdom and insight regarding the final book cover.

To Cynthia Stillar for her professionalism and high touch style in positioning the book for publication.

Prologue
LIFE ISN'T EASY

We pass and review on the center stage of life
Just one time, not knowing what a new day might bring.

A broken heart, a crushed spirit, a shattered dream,
Trusting that someday the sun will shine again with a new song to sing.

When a crisis looms on the horizon,
It will never telegraph its arrival by knocking on your door.
It will strike suddenly, unexpectedly, and at times it will be catastrophic,
Leaving you with unanswered questions to explore.

A major failure, defeat, or disappointment is not fatal, nor is it final,
And that is something you must believe.
The very next chapter awaiting you
Will take you on an uncharted course with exciting
        accomplishments to achieve.

Don't give up in the game of life, for it's always too soon to quit.
Keep holding on with strength and courage,
It's not easy, I admit.

But when you do and maintain your vision,
Keeping a strong faith and passion for what you do,
Remember your tears and pain will never be wasted and
        I can promise you, that God will see you through.

Introduction
IF LIFE ISN'T EASY,
THEN IT MUST BE HARD

"Why," you may be wondering, "does a book about integrity start off with all this talk about life being hard? I just need to know how to live the right way!"

There's a very important reason I begin this book by reminding you (and me!) that life is hard. Yes, I want to encourage, challenge, and direct you to live a life of integrity. But integrity doesn't happen in a vacuum. The choices you make that define whether or not you're living with integrity don't arrive on the scene in a perfect world. Everything you do—and that means everything that determines your level of integrity—happens right in the middle of the hardness of life. In truth, living with integrity is one of the hard things in life. If integrity were easy, you wouldn't need a book to tell you how to do it. And I wouldn't have had so many hard lessons that taught me what I hope to teach you.

Have you ever experienced in real life your worst nightmare? I have.

My life was neatly arranged—success in business, an all-American family, good friends, health. In short, I felt bullet-proof. I was lulled into believing that truly bad things in life "could never happen to me." Yet one stupid mistake turned my world upside down. I traded a short-term gain for some very long-term pain, and that, by all standards, is a devastating trade-off.

The bad news I discovered and must pass on to you is that success is not permanent. But the good news is that a major failure, defeat, or disappointment is not fatal, nor is it final. In the future, when you experience a "dark hour," let the principles and examples in this book guide you to getting your life back.

If you sincerely intend to live with integrity, you can't approach the subject with even a shred of excuse about how you live. You must have a "no-excuse" mentality. You can't think for a moment, "Oh, I would do that if not for this (or that) particular hard issue in my life." Things are as they are, and that means it is often hard—very hard—to live with integrity. But the great secret of this and every other godly hard thing in life is that once you determine to live with integrity, your long-term happiness is secured. And that makes life just a little bit easier.

THE INSIDER'S GUIDE TO INTEGRITY

An astounding number of people in America have one foot in prison and don't even know it. They flirt with gray areas that grow gradually darker until what was once gray looks almost white, and black is no longer so murky. The allure of living "on the edge" promises self-realization but delivers self-destruction for most who try it. The "fudge factor" creeps into thought processes that translate into lie-based living.

America's principle of self-government grew out of a way of life advocated by our Founding Fathers. It didn't leap from nowhere onto the law books to direct our system of government. It began as the recognition that each individual should take full responsibility for his or her actions, decisions, and their consequences. Only through individual responsibility could a government "by the people" hope to succeed.

Unfortunately, "selective integrity" is sweeping America. Crooked accounting practices, phony earnings reports, corporate fraud, complacent boards of directors, and misused funds are just a sampling of how people try to beat the system. And, of course, selective integrity is really no integrity at all. As from our founding roots, though, living with complete integrity, taking full responsibility, starts with what's inside each individual.

If you want to live a life of integrity, it's essential to know where you're starting on the "selective integrity scale." So ask yourself: Beyond the walls of my home and my church, does my life demand an explanation? Is your way of life consistent from one place to another, or do you have to continuously explain (perhaps just to yourself, sometimes to others) why you're doing what you're doing? Consistency helps define the level of integrity with which you live. The Bible says, "a double-minded man is unstable in all his ways" (James 1:8, KJV).

Integrity is an "inside job." When your inner moral compass is alive and well, you won't compromise, negotiate, or violate your integrity. You pay attention to what's below the surface in your life because that's what drives your actions.

I warned you to start with that life is hard because the greatest challenge to integrity usually comes when a hard choice raises its head. Making the honest choice—above reproach—often is not the alternative with the most apparent short-term payoff. But long-term success swings on the hinges of integrity. Integrity will stand the test of time and survive the very closest scrutiny.

When you make integrity the cornerstone upon which you build your life, you will simplify the present and un-complicate your future.

Chapter 1

INTEGRITY—YOUR BIGGEST CHALLENGE

One of the most gripping human tragedies of all time is the story of the HMS *Titanic*. The most splendid ship ever built—in many ways not surpassed even now, nearly a century after its heartbreaking demise—sank midway through its first voyage because the crew failed to pay attention to dangers below the water's surface. The *Titanic* received a series of iceberg warnings, the sixth of which came through just after midnight on that ill-fated morning. The radio operator on duty wired back, "Shut up! I'm busy." And thirty minutes later the submerged mountain of a North Atlantic iceberg gashed open the underbelly of the great ship, whose captain had said, "Even God could not sink this awesome vessel." In less than three hours, most of its crew and passengers were drowned and the rest adrift in the frigid waters. What had happened? They forgot the truth about icebergs. What they could see above the surface of the water could not sink this marvelous ship, but the 90% below the surface could send any ship to the bottom of the sea.

That iceberg is a metaphor for your life. Ten percent above the surface of the water is your reputation. The 90% below the surface is your character, and if integrity is not part of your character, that 90% can sink your personal ship. "Sinking" happens most often when life is at its hardest.

THE DEADLY TRIANGLE

Eighty-five percent of white-collar crime in America happens because three integrity-challenging factors converge, creating what I call the "deadly triangle." First, a person finds him or herself in dire financial need—overused credit, a risky investment gone bad, a divorce, or some other personal financial catastrophe. Second, his or her job or business has placed the person in a position to have the "perfect cover-up" for wrongdoing, so there's little fear of getting caught for stealing, embezzling, or monkeying with finances. Finally, the person is angry or resentful over an unfulfilled promise of a pay raise or promotion, and he or she can feel justified in getting something the company "owed me anyway." The deadly triangle will overwhelm virtually anyone not prepared in advance to withstand the temptation to do wrong. Only integrity with its long-term payoff can hope to forestall the short-term gain promised by closet wrongdoings.

Integrity and character go hand in hand. Character is what you do in the dark when no one else is watching. It is the ability to do what is right even if you don't feel like it. Character involves embracing godly core values—principles you stand by amidst the pressures and hardness of everyday life.

There's never been any mystery about why people call me Basketball Bill. I love basketball. To me, it's the greatest sport, pastime, game, or diversion ever created by man. And its heroes are my greatest heroes, so I must tell you about a man who will for years to come be revered as the finest coach the sport has ever produced—and a model of character and integrity.

John Wooden, legendary coach of the UCLA Bruins and the man ESPN dubbed "Coach of the Century," stood firmly by the necessity of good character. Regardless of an athlete's drive and ability, he often claimed that "talent will take you to the top, but it will take character to keep you there." Wooden never fixated on winning or losing. He stressed the fundamentals of basketball and the essential character trait required to succeed: Every athlete must be a consummate team player. A team player always elevates the performance of everyone else, and there is no limit to what a team can achieve if it doesn't matter who gets the credit. Let me illustrate.

Wooden insisted on giving credit where credit is due. In basketball, nothing sets up a score better than a well-timed, smartly-thrown pass. And on Coach Wooden's team, if one player received a great pass and made a sensational basket that brought the house down, he was required to immediately acknowledge the player who made the pass. If he didn't, no matter what scoring streak he might be running, that player would find himself sitting out the rest of the game—even in a championship!—on the bench. In Coach Wooden's world, nothing trumped the principles of character. His commitment—and the follow-through it rendered—held every players' attention. It promoted harmony, which led to cooperation, which led to teamwork, which led to unmatched success. At one time, UCLA held an 88-game winning streak, a record that still stands more than 20 years after Coach Wooden's retirement. The team won ten NCAA championships, seven of which were consecutive—another feat that remains unsurpassed. Wooden put character and the associated integrity above winning. He required his players to set aside the short-term self-gratification of taking all the glory of a

good shot, but look what they got in return: The once-in-many-
lifetimes privilege of participating in the most successful college
basketball dynasty of all time!

INTEGRITY EVERY DAY

As much as I live and breathe basketball, I have to admit there
are excellent examples of integrity from all walks of life. Even
though I'm discouraged by the lack of integrity I often see or read
about (it makes the most profitable news), I'm also encouraged
by the people I've consulted with, spoken to, and taught in some
of America's finest corporations. While I'm usually supposed
to be the teacher, I've gleaned many gems of wisdom about
integrity from those I've worked with, and I'd like to share some
of them with you. Here are some definitions of integrity from
top business leaders:

- Walking your talk.
- Telling the truth as fast as you can.
- Doing a "gut" check: If I do this today, will I embarrass
  my family tomorrow?
- Living each day with honor. Honoring your word,
  honoring commitments, and honoring relationships—in
  other words, being an honorable person.
- Being a person of the highest integrity, even in the face of
  personal disaster.
- Striving for moral soundness by living above reproach.
  Reaching down for every fiber within you to be squeaky
  clean. You're not for sale at any price.

What's so great about these leaders is that they do what they
say they should do. They relish the advantage of living with
integrity.

PRESERVING THE SAINTS

Integrity and salt have something in common: They both preserve. Psalm 25:21 (NKJV) says, "Let integrity and uprightness preserve me for I wait for You," and Jesus called His disciples the salt of the earth. For centuries, until the invention of refrigeration technology, salt was the basic form of preservative for foods that would otherwise rot, and many of us need to get back to the basics so we can experience the preservative benefits of integrity. Right-living will preserve you from disaster.

The Enron Energy and Worldcom scandals represent what happens when the preserving quality of integrity is ignored. Those involved were overwhelmed by the temptation to generate personal fortunes by inflating stock prices. Rather than report company profits honestly, they manipulated accounting practices, and as the end of the story shows, the price for their dishonesty was higher than any they received for their stock options.

The head of a non-profit organization, who was a theologian by training, once probed a business executive: "My organization hired an accountant to keep our books straight, so why doesn't your organization hire a theologian to keep your ethics straight?" Not a bad idea for bolstering a company's integrity.

Sadly, the problem of selective integrity is not restricted to top executives. Studies show that roughly 25% of all employees in America are stealing one of four things from their employer: time, information, money, or inventory. No one is immune from the temptation to compromise integrity.

About this selective integrity that is sweeping America: Test yourself to see if you're being sucked in by asking, "When was the last time you shaded the truth ever so slightly in order to get what you want?"

To exaggerate beyond the truth is all too common. It is tempting to embellish the facts regarding something a person desperately wants, such as:

(1) Résumé fraud. Experts tell us 42% of job hunters submit résumés that misrepresent themselves and omit facts.

(2) Financial statements. Fudge a little in order to get that new car loan or home mortgage.

(3) Tax returns. Someone might think, "No one is looking over my shoulder. Therefore I can get away with what I'm filing."

(4) Expense accounts. A salesperson is denied a pay raise so he or she thinks padding an expense report is justified.

(5) Athletes in high school and college cheat on exams because they "have given so much to their sport."

Most people will face some form of pressure every day and need the preservation from temptation that integrity provides. In the political arena there is pressure to keep constituents happy at all costs in order to assure re-election. In the corporate world there is pressure to ring up more sales with greater profits than the year before. In both amateur and professional athletics there is pressure to win. In the classroom there is pressure to excel in academics. For teenagers and adults alike there is peer pressure.

People generally don't realize that when they compromise, they give away part of themselves. They begin living on other people's terms, basing decisions on the expectations of others rather than on their own good judgment. Trading short-term gain for long-term pain is always a lousy trade-off. I never cease to be amazed how ordinary people can find themselves in extraordinary trouble. Doctors, lawyers, certified public accountants, educators, preachers, priests, law enforcement officials, business executives, professional athletes, blue-collar workers, students, legislators, governors, and federal judges, all bring countless troubles upon themselves because they lack integrity. So how do you avoid becoming one of the crowd of compromisers?

SIX MISTAKES THAT LEAD TO COMPROMISED INTEGRITY

No one is immune to making a major mistake that goes public, but you can improve your odds of staying out of the painful limelight by recognizing mistakes before you make them. Here are six key errors you can see coming. Avoid them!

(1) Blind-side mistakes. Multi-lane highways are designed to make it easier to change lanes and pass slow-moving vehicles, but have you ever been cruising one of the five lanes, decide to move over thinking all is clear, yet as you change lanes a horn blares "out of nowhere"? What happened? That sports car or Harley was hidden in your blind spot. Of course, you swerve to avoid an accident, but evasive action would never have been needed if you had just taken one quick glance over your shoulder to check the spot your mirrors don't show. Life is full of blind spots that a little extra care will reveal. Even when you think "all is clear," take another glance around.

(2) Stupid mistakes. Have you ever made a stupid mistake? Of course. It would take another whole book for me to tell you all the ones I've made, but the really hard-to-face question is: Have you made the same stupid mistake more than once? Ouch! It happens to people all the time. You wonder: "How did I manage to do that again?" You question your intelligence and your sanity. Well, quit beating yourself up, and exercise more common sense the next time. Good judgment and common sense go hand in hand. Practice avoiding little stupid mistakes, so

you don't make the big ones that can really mess up your life.

(3) Peer pressure mistakes. We usually associate peer pressure with young people—especially teenagers—but the truth is, no one likes rejection, especially by our peers. Peer pressure is an ordeal because we all long to be needed, wanted, appreciated, and accepted. In one way or another, the central challenge of peer pressure is, "I dare you." You accept the dare—whatever the risk to your integrity. But for this potential mistake, "Just say 'No'" applies.

(4) Panic-induced mistakes. When you panic, your rational mind isn't working for you. Everything is a reaction. All you think about is survival in the here and now. There is no future. You throw out good decision-making skills, and like a rabbit by the roadside that darts under your tires at the last second, your panic obliterates your chances of surviving whatever problem you face. If you ever feel yourself starting to panic, just stop. Whatever you're inclined to do, don't do it. Stop until you can get control of yourself and make a rational choice.

(5) Poor judgment mistakes. When faced with making a decision, it's common to rationalize what you want from your own limited point of view. It takes discipline to get "outside of yourself," to really hear the good counsel of worthy advisors, and do what is best—even if it takes you out of your comfort zone. When you listen to your inner voice, listen only to positive reinforcement! Being comfortable is not always being right. You can make easy decisions, fast decisions, smart decisions, or slow, well-thought-out ones. Proverbs 21:5 gives a big hint about which is best: "Good planning and hard work lead to prosperity, but hasty shortcuts lead to poverty" (NLT). The

consequences of "haste makes waste" usually accompany poor judgment.

(6) Not-facing-the-facts mistakes. This could also be called "Don't confuse me with the facts, my mind is already made up" mistakes. Having a runaway ego and the accompanying overdose of pride will trigger reckless and sloppy decision-making and will put you on a collision course with disaster. Some people won't seek help from a friend who has wisdom, insight, and discernment. They think they know it all. To put it simply: Don't be one of them. Gather all the pertinent facts, and then pay attention to what the facts tell you.

So if these are possible ways to "get it wrong," how do you get it right?

THREE STORIES OF DOING IT RIGHT

Michael Jordan, superstar of the NBA champion Chicago Bulls and reputed by sports experts to be the best professional basketball player in history, was featured in a national TV commercial a few years ago. He observes, "In my career I've missed over 9,000 shots." Jordan goes on to admit, "I've lost 300 ball games. Twenty-six times I was asked by my coach to take the final shot to win the game for my team, and all 26 times I failed, but through my many failures I now succeed." What can we gain from this commercial? Michael Jordan learned to attach value to failure. The value he places on failure takes away his fear of it, and that allows him to stay with his integrity.

Here's another Michael Jordan example (I love basketball and its heroes, remember?). In one game at the peak of Michael's career he scored only nine points against an arch rival, and this at a time when he had been averaging 30 points per game. A reporter charged Michael after the game to ask, "Michael Jordan, what is wrong with you? You didn't even make double digits—for the first time this season?" Consistent with his "no excuse mentality," Michael replied straightforwardly, "I can't walk on water. I had a bad day. I had a bad game. I have no more to say." End of interview. What a man willing to take responsibility! What an American!

Just so you'll know there's room in Basketball Bill's heart for folks other than athletes, I'll also tell you a story about someone from another group I love. I speak with business executives almost every day, and the good ones—of which there are many!—unfortunately often find themselves maligned along with the bad ones. That's one reason why the James E. Casey story is so important. He shows that men of character in business leadership do some of the greatest service of any people anywhere.

In 1907, at age 19, James Casey founded the United Parcel Service with a $100 bill and big dreams for his upstart business in Seattle, Washington. His best friend chided him, "James, you're not going to make it in your new business. There are eight major competitors in this city that are going to eat your lunch."

To that, James responded forthrightly, "I'm not only going to survive. I'm going to thrive in my new little business. The two reasons? For the most part, my competitors will be people of integrity most of the time, but we will be people of integrity all the time. My competition will also give quality service most of the time, but we will give quality service 100% of the time."

In recent years, UPS has laid claim to being the "tightest ship in the shipping business." But is it? As they say, the best compliment is the one that comes from a third party, and after Mr. Casey died in 1983, the March 1988 *Congressional Record* paid him a wonderful tribute by quoting him and his vision for integrity: "We have become known by all those who deal with us as people of integrity, and that priceless asset is the most valuable thing we possess."

Yes, integrity to Mr. Casey was more important than the vast jet fleet, more important than its 18-wheelers on the open road, more important than the small brown trucks scurrying around town, and more important than hundreds of free-standing hubs across America that store the ground vehicles overnight. Doubtless the company founder's priority commitment to character is a major reason UPS is still one of America's premiere companies after 100 years of service.

INTEGRITY STARTS AT HOME

Home is a good laboratory for getting things right that you want to apply in other areas of life. But it's also the most important "end user" of good character. If the way you live "works" on the home front, it will work on every other front. And often the rewards at home are greater than any you could dream of somewhere else. Let me give you a personal example of how I found this out.

When my daughter Noelle was a teenager, I was put to the consistency test. I had always told my family the importance of keeping your word, but not even I realized how much it matters to make sure I always keep mine.

One evening, I received a phone call from a new client who had just booked me to speak at three regional sales conferences. I was to give a 2-hour sales symposium at each location—a big deal for me, to say the least, since keynotes like this are hard to come by. When he called, my client was on a 3-hour layover at the Dallas/Ft. Worth airport on his way to California. He invited me to join him at the airport Hyatt Regency Hotel for what would have been some very fine dining. He wanted to discuss the theme of the sales conferences as well as sales strategies for each regional meeting. Without hesitating, I responded with what some people would consider a very bad business move: "Sir, thank you for your invitation, but I'll have to take a rain check. I have made a prior commitment for 7:00 this evening." Besides missing the chance to discuss our upcoming event, I suspect my client was disappointed at having to enjoy his fine dinner alone, but he understood and agreed to get together at a later date.

When I hung up, Noelle said, "Dad, I overheard your conversation, and I'm wondering: Is that the new client you told mom and me about last week?"

After I told her it was indeed that client, Noelle continued, "Why did you say 'no' to him and a fancy dinner at the Hyatt?"

"The answer is simple," I said. "It's because I had a prior engagement tonight with a special young lady named Candi Noelle Chaffin. We're going shopping together to get her a new pair of shoes and a dress."

"Wow!" Noelle exclaimed, "I must be pretty important to my daddy."

Of course, I assured her that she is very important to me. But I've told her that many times. What made this particular incident significant is that this time I showed her by my actions that she is important.

Well, we didn't just go shopping. We went what I call shopping-ping-ping-ping—for 2-1/2 hours we shopping'ed. Noelle was very thorough and deliberate until she found what she wanted, and we capped off our special time together with a yogurt treat.

At our table in the yogurt shop Noelle returned to our earlier conversation: "Dad, if you had said 'yes' to that man tonight and 'no' to me, you would have taken a giant step backwards in our father-daughter relationship. However, you made a very smart decision when you honored your word and reserved the evening for me."

Now it was my turn for a
worth that kind of affirmati
I did was to do what I said

The lesson was espec
than two years, I had beer
whatever reason, she didn
had seen what was going
encouraged me: "Keep gi
her unconditionally." I c
broke whatever barrier h

When we returned home from the shopping center,
carefully stowed the shoes and dress in her room, then came
running into the den and blurted, "Hey Dad I forgot something."
My precious daughter threw her arms around me and kissed me
on the cheek. "Thanks, Dad, for making tonight so special," she
said with tears flowing down her cheeks.

I caught Kay's sparkling eye as she peeked into the room, and
I wanted to hold on to that moment forever. So I ask you, parents:
Have you ever given one-way hugs to a son or daughter? If so, I
plead with you to keep on giving them. And keep your word at
home. There is no more rewarding place to start. Remember: As
the home front goes, so goes the business.

In every sport, there are boundaries and rules to play by, but
in golf, they sometimes seem especially merciless. When you
violate them, you can lose your ball entirely and bring the game
to a complete halt until you give up looking for it and take your
penalty shot. I love to imagine what would happen in America if
we got used to playing within healthy boundaries once again—
if we got back to the truth in politics, truth in selling, truth in
lending, truth in the media, truth in advertising, being truthful
with co-workers, being truthful with family members, but most
important being honest with yourself. In fact, in the next chapter,
I'll tell you more about what I imagine that America would look

personal story that shattered my world.
nce that challenged every shred of integrity
art my personal world, but taught me how to
never lose it again.

S...CAMERAS...DISASTER

MY MOTION PICTURE STORY—PART 1

The glitter, riches, and window dressing of Hollywood appear gratifying, fun, exhilarating, and desirable. What you see, though, is not always what you get—a lesson I learned the (very) hard way.

As I neared the pinnacle of my first career—as a marketing executive and consultant—I didn't have the wisdom to know there are some challenges that are simply way too big for me. At the time, I didn't believe anything could be too tough for me to handle. I was convinced by my successes that I could do most anything I set my mind to. And sometimes that's not a bad attitude to have, but it can get you into trouble if it's not tempered by some good sense.

My problems started early one morning with a phone call I thought would fling me into a new world of success. A CPA friend asked if I would consider getting involved with a movie project that needed help. His introduction to the task sounded exciting— especially to a dyed-in-the-wool sports lover like me. The film was to feature four superstars from the Dallas Cowboys: Ed "Too Tall" Jones, Drew Pearson, Jay Saldi, and Thomas "Hollywood" Henderson. Happy to spend time with anyone who had just won the Super Bowl, I quickly agreed to meet with the players and my friend's accounting firm.

After three hours with the football stars, I leaped at their suggestion that I become the film's executive producer. What season-ticket-holding Cowboys fanatic wouldn't have had his ego stroked by that kind of offer? I was happy to let the accounting firm think my "movie mogul" experience with the dog movie Benji qualified me for the tempestuous job they needed done. In truth, all I had done for Benji was to play tennis with the puppy's executive producer, invest a few dollars in the proposition, watch a handful of location scenes in the making, and attend the movie's world premiere. I'd never even petted the star himself! Nevertheless, the wondrous trappings of Hollywood and four Super Bowl heroes lured me into something I had no business taking part in. I convinced myself I could take someone else's mess, convert it into a financial bonanza for everyone involved, and be the hero to several of my heroes. In reality, my runaway ego was as big as Texas.

On June 15, 1978, I started bailing out the sinking ship called Squeeze Play. (We spelled "squeeze" with two "z's" instead of a double "e" to emphasize the tight spot in which the main characters find themselves. It was an ironic foreshadowing of my own predicament.) Bear in mind that a normal business strategy for a film requires the final script in hand, a completed storyboard, all locations tied down, and the entire budget in an escrow account before a single frame of film is exposed. On the day the production crew arrived to meet their new leader, not one of these key elements was in place. When the Hollywood crew—including a veteran director—arrived in Dallas, the plans I had inherited gave us exactly 30 days to shoot every scene in which the Dallas players were to appear. In a month, the fantastic four were off to the Thousand Oaks training camp to prepare for the upcoming NFL season, and key players on a Super Bowl team simply weren't given time off to shoot movies.

Standing in front of a critical-looking group in a meeting room at Dallas's Northpark Inn, my introduction at our first production meeting wasn't very elegant. "Good morning everyone. I'm Bill Chaffin, your executive producer for Squeeze Play. What time do we actually begin shooting today?"

"What do you mean when do we begin shooting," snarled one of the crew, "the real question is where are we going to shoot?"

Brilliant soul that I am, I knew immediately we had a problem. Fortunately, I was introduced that morning to a local producer who immediately became a bright spot in the dim scene. I hired her that day to orchestrate our daily tasks—location selection, screening potential actors and actresses for bit parts, acquiring costumes, retaining make-up specialists, even enrolling the caterer to make sure a hungry crew had plenty to eat. While she was on the scene, I was behind it, scrambling to raise the $530,000 budget I had filed with the Secretary of State in Austin. Little by little the magnitude of my responsibility became clear. My "elite" position as executive producer meant I was also the general partner to a limited motion picture partnership—which meant I assumed all the risk of the venture! I was in the real estate and insurance industry for 24 years, and I always examined the risk factors. This was critical in order to represent my clients' best interests. However, in this case I had a blind side. Because I controlled the checkbook, I didn't think there was any risk. That was pure folly on my part, of course, thinking I had all the answers. On top of that, our critical path was so critical we could not afford even a single day of rain in the shooting schedule. We faced a championship-level, must-win situation every day.

The Hollywood team insisted Squezze Play *would have to be an R-rated picture to succeed. I disagreed and steadfastly determined to put wholesome entertainment on the silver screens that would show my movie. A PG rating would have to do. I eliminated sexual scenes, violence, and abusive language, but my decisions added greatly to the misunderstandings and communication breakdowns that plagued our group.*

I realized the discontent had come to a head the time I received a late-night phone call from the director of our lighting crew. In slurred, drunken speech, he threatened, "Mr. Chaffin, the word is out that you might miss payroll. If you miss payroll tomorrow, you won't be using your knuckles any more."

A chill surged up and down my spine. No one had ever threatened me with bodily harm, and the seriousness of the situation held my undivided attention through a completely sleepless night. Many problems that I inherited were never fully resolved, and I managed to go over budget on the film by $300,000, but one thing was for sure—I never missed payroll.

At this point in my story, I'd like to pause for a moment to explain what I now recognize was going on in my life. There are seven problems that can lead to failure in any enterprise, and I had all seven working on me in Squezze Play:

(1) A runaway ego puts you on a collision course with disaster.

(2) Thinking you have all the answers is always a false estimate of your capability.

(3) Having no experience or knowledge of the task at hand is a serious deficit.

(4) Greed and power without accountability corrupt.

(5) Being cocky and arrogant blinds you to problems.

(6) Being full of excuses when things don't go right keeps you from solving problems.

(7) All the above lead to defective decision-making.

The decisions we make determine the path we take, and many times the most intense pain results from self-inflicted wounds. And I made the wounds deeper with every day on the Squezze Play *set.*

Someone could create a great motion picture comedy about the making of Squezze Play, *but we managed to get the four players' footage in the can by July 15. We did the post-production at MGM in Culver City, California, eventually trimming 90,000 feet of film to 9,000—an hour-and-a-half feature film destined (so we thought) for theaters across America.*

The Reader's Digest *version of the script goes like this. Four football players return home from the Vietnam War and try to fit back into society. They re-enroll in school, hoping college football will be a springboard to a professional career. Their Psychology*

101 professor, a dazzling former co-ed engaged to a Harvard law student, steals the heart of Jay Saldi, and a triangle romance begins. To complicate the relationship further, the professor's father is a wealthy but crooked politician who sells firearms illegally to foreign countries. The war veteran football players become heroes again by bringing the bad guy to ruin. It wasn't Gone with the Wind, but on a scale of 1 to 10, the film made it to 5.

In the end, everyone involved turned in remarkable performances. The musical score was breathtaking, thanks to my good friend, Gary Vacca, a musician from SMU who wrote, produced, arranged, and sang most of the songs in the picture. Gary even acted alongside the football players. Our photography was marvelous, and the four Dallas Cowboys were very credible actors.

Jay Saldi played the male lead, and I still admire the intensity of his drive to learn his part and play with enthusiasm and focus. During a key football scene, Drew Pearson, one of the best wide receivers in Dallas history, made some of the most spectacular one-hand catches I'd ever seen. "Too Tall" Jones and "Hollywood" Henderson delivered some unbelievable stunts and several hilarious scenes. (Thanks, guys!)

Getting the film from camera to the theater, though, is when I first began to sense that this project was not going to have a happy ending. Along the way, everything cost more than I had imagined it could, but post-production expenses were the most astounding of all to a neophyte like me. One day I challenged MGM on some of their charges, and the executive on the phone knew instantly what I was all about. "Bill Chaffin," he chided, "this must be your first motion picture." And I had thought I was so smart!

Beginning to realize just how far in over my head I was, I prayed every day that God would give me wisdom, discernment, and direction in handling the cascade of challenges that just wouldn't end. The key to the movie's launch and possibly its ultimate success was to be the world premiere on June 15, one year to the day after *that first production meeting at the Northpark Inn. We had already reserved the Chateau Theater in Irving, Texas, when I called MGM and asked them for a film print to show at the debut. I don't know if that same executive had been expecting my call, but they delivered another sucker punch to the first-timer from Dallas. A film print, I learned, is never sent out until all the post-production bills are paid, and at the time I still owed MGM $60,000—about 60,000 times more than I had in the bank. I was out of money and also out of ideas.*

> **BILL'S HARD LESSON #1**
>
> **SHARPEN YOUR DECISION-MAKING SKILLS, AND THINK TWICE BEFORE YOU LEAP.**

Chapter 2

THE CONFIDENCE OF INTEGRITY

A motivational speaker for more than 20 years, I've probably logged a half-million miles of airline travel. Long drives to the airport, interminable waits for a parking shuttle, laborious car rentals, terminal congestion, and seemingly endless days en route to somewhere else are common fare for me. Perhaps fun for the novice, long-distance travel can be a loathsome waste of life for a veteran. But one man has redeemed that waste for thousands of corporate flyers over the last 40 years.

THE SKY'S (JUST BARELY) THE LIMIT

An inventor, pilot, and business leader in the 1950s, Bill Lear envisioned a stunning new concept in travel when he imagined building a high-speed, "personal-sized" jet airplane. By the time he started to develop what we now know as the Lear Jet, Bill already held more than 150 patents including the automatic pilot, the car radio, and 8-track tapes (don't laugh—they were an impressive innovation at the time!).

Through all my miles in the sky, I've had only two chances to fly in a Lear Jet, and the first time was breathtaking. If all it had done were to cut my travel time in half (no ticket counters, long-term parking lots, or boarding passes), I would have loved the flight. But the most magic series of moments began as I stepped through the passenger door and into the fuselage of Bill Lear's marvelous creation. This serene, cushioned tube with jet engines strapped to the outside offered an insulated world, safe from the abuses of routine travel for a half dozen fortunate people. I felt the exhilaration of a fighter pilot (at least according to my imagination) as the takeoff thrust pinned me to my seat. We slid through the atmosphere, and for the first time in years, I was sorry the flight was over so soon.

Bill Lear's fantastic invention, though, is alive and thriving today only because of this man's integrity and the high price he paid to preserve it. Turning his dream into reality took years, but in 1963 the prototype Lear Jet took its maiden flight. By 1964, Mr. Lear delivered his first jet to a client, and the plane was an immediate and stunning business success. In short order, 55 Lears crisscrossed the country for executives in several dozen corporations. But into Bill Lear's euphoric beginning entered two gut-wrenching tragedies.

A pair of the glittering new jets crashed inexplicably. Lear was personally devastated, and despite the threat of disastrous publicity that could scuttle the early success of his dream-built company, Lear immediately sent word to all jet owners to ground their planes until he and his team could determine what had caused the mishaps. The possibility that more lives might be lost was far more important to him than any adverse publicity the grounding of his planes might generate.

As he researched the ill-fated flights, Lear isolated a likely cause, but he could not verify the technical problem on the ground. The only way to determine whether or not he had diagnosed the malfunction correctly would be to recreate the crash scenarios—in the air. A potentially lethal undertaking, Lear insisted on conducting the test himself. As he rocketed through the sky, he nearly lost control and barely escaped the same fate as the two unsuspecting pilots who had crashed. But he verified the defect and developed a new part to correct the problem. Lear fitted the remaining 53 planes with the compensating piece and eliminated the danger.

Not only did grounding the planes and fixing the problem cost Lear huge profits and nearly his own life, it planted doubt about his innovative aircraft in the minds of potential customers. Although it took Lear two years to rebuild his badly shaken business, he never regretted his decision. To solve the mystery of those crashes, he was willing to risk his success, his fortune, and even his life—but not his integrity.

Lear knew that sometimes the biggest risk is taking no risk at all. There are some things over which you have no control, but you can always control your integrity. Every time you choose to act with integrity, you give the quality of your character an upgrade.

At the end of the last chapter, I promised to tell you what I think lives of integrity and character lived throughout America would look like. In a word, I would describe them as "confident." Bill Lear made tough choices but could live in confidence that he walked with integrity. He would always be able to look his fellow man in the eye.

THE CHEMISTRY OF CONFIDENCE

In his superb book, *The Success Syndrome*, Harvard Medical School psychologist Steven Berglas observes that "people who achieve great height, but lack the bedrock character to sustain them through stressful circumstances, are headed for disaster." He believes they are destined for one or more of the four catastrophic A's: Arrogance, painful Aloneness, self-destructive Adventure-seeking, or Adultery. Each comes with a high price.

Your actions demonstrate your character, and they must match up if you're going to be known as a reliable and dependable person, as someone who influences others for the better. Executives of the "highest integrity" and "sterling character" take on a responsibility beyond what their job descriptions demand. There is an implied expectation to model integrity and solid character.

A highly successful friend of mine hung in his office an oil painting depicting an elderly man with head bowed over a simple meal. My friend bought the picture because, as he told an associate, "I want to keep this in front of me as a reminder to remain humble." This man understood the necessity of maintaining a godly perspective on himself. Every executive suite in America should have outside the door a caution sign in flashing red lights: "Warning—Large doses of success can undermine your marriage, wipe out your family life, destroy your health, ruin your business, and leave the path behind you strewn with broken relationships."

A key to guarding against losing perspective is to always make it a point to under-promise and over-deliver. Be humble enough to tell others you can accomplish less than you really hope you can, but work to achieve far more. When you dazzle people by doing even more than you say you will, a special chemistry develops. Others will see that your actions spring from an honest heart, and they will reward you with unconditional support. When you act with pure motives, people believe what you say. They will be loyal, willing to do what you want. They will trust and follow you, and isn't that what any leader—business, political, or church—wants? The under-promise, over-deliver formula is powerful! Model this principle, and employees at every level can embrace it. If your whole organization under-promises and over-delivers, you can bet it will impact your bottom line dramatically.

INTEGRITY, THE REPUTATION OF CHOICE

Proverbs 16:11 directs people to "be fair in all your business dealings" (Living Bible). Giving a "square deal" means finding a win-win situation for everyone involved. People are drawn to anyone who can craft a situation from which they will benefit, and once you have a reputation for creating wins, you'll have others calling you to get on board with your business.

A long-standing example of an everyone-wins organization is Tiffany and Company. Tiffany's has an immaculate reputation for "delivering the goods" because of a determination to do it right time and time again. When you buy a diamond or a string of pearls from Tiffany's, you're sure to get the finest quality jewelry possible.

A good reputation cannot be assumed. It must be earned. When you give more value than people expect, it will benefit your growth, permanency, and profits—a pretty good strategy if you want to stay in business for the long haul. As I like to tell my audiences, "What gets you there will keep you there."

Surprisingly, people can also be very forgiving if they know you always intend to act with integrity. Everyone makes mistakes, and everyone knows that. When you make a mistake, people will likely forgive you, but only when they have no doubt about your integrity. Those with less natural ability and high integrity will accomplish far more than people with greater natural ability and less integrity.

Way back (and I do mean way back) when I was ten years old, my mother pointed out, "Billy, always tell the truth. That way you'll never have to remember what you say." Telling the complete truth 100% of the time means you never have to pile lie upon lie to cover up a "truth gap." No matter how little the gap may be at first, it will widen until it swallows your life.

President Eisenhower once offered his opinion on integrity: "In order to be a leader a man must have followers. And to have followers, a man must have confidence. Hence, the supreme quality for a leader is unquestionably integrity."

George Washington observed that "few men have the virtue to withstand the highest bidder." It's amazing how many people can be bought. Yet the best way to guard against a breach of integrity is to decide today that you won't sell your integrity for any reason—not for power, revenge, pride, or money. Choose the path of integrity if you want to walk confidently wherever you go.

THINK WITH INTEGRITY

Integrity begins in your thoughts. The quality of your thought life is a precise indicator of your character. Integrity commits itself to character over personal gain, to people over things, to service over power, to principle over convenience, and to the long view over the immediate. Making these decisions for integrity is a thought process you must cultivate.

Your thought life will determine your level of success. When you bring every thought captive, you discipline your mind to dwell only on things that are pure, powerful, noble, and positive. The other side is unseemly, polluted, weak, and negative. Despite what some people would like to think, you cannot straddle the fence, sampling "just a few" of the morsels from the dirty side. You're on one side or the other. You're for God and His holiness or against Him. If you see that you're on the wrong side (or in the middle!) just get over it—back to the good. Change is inevitable, so make it positive. When you change for the good, an awesome thing happens. Your character wins.

Flawed character, on the other hand, is a person's internal moral "fault line." Place enough stress on the crack, and an earthquake happens. Living in gray areas and allowing the "fudge factor" to take over will generate the moral cracks. If you let them go on, the tremors of life will eventually trigger an 8.2 quake on the moral Richter scale. Some people spend years digging out from the rubble of a moral disaster, and often their recovery is slowed because too few ever admit they are responsible for the mess they made. What happened is their fault.

Harry Stonecipher, chief executive of Boeing, one of America's largest aircraft manufacturers and defense contractors, was the architect of his company's ethics policy. Yet just after he and his wife celebrated their golden wedding anniversary, the company's board of directors asked him to resign. Why? They discovered Mr. Stonecipher had been having an affair with a female Boeing executive, 20 years younger than he. Stonecipher's thoughts most likely followed the line that since he lived in Chicago and she in Washington, D.C., no one would find out what he was doing in private, more than 700 miles from home.

All of us live in three worlds: public, family, and private. And the most private world is our thoughts. Mr. Stonecipher ignored the truth that anything we do—positive or negative—in our private worlds will eventually surface in the other two, no matter how clever the plan to keep it a secret.

Usually if people do something they know is wrong, it's because they believe they have the perfect cover-up. The glitch in Mr. Stonecipher's plan was that an e-mail to his lady friend found its way to a board member, and his perfect cover was blown. But think about it. If there's any cover you'll even consider using to get away with something, your integrity is out the window already. Keeping your thoughts in line is crucial to walking in integrity. Mr. Stonecipher's poor judgment had an enormous cost. He lost a monumental salary with "all the perks" and his wife of 50 years.

Wisdom is the nurturing of thoughts that produce good character, that avoid or heal a moral fault zone. Wisdom allows you to live skillfully, knowing and doing right, and to live our life from God's point of view. A wise person recognizes that no individual has all the answers. Gaining wisdom requires asking questions of others and revering God. Scripture says, "The fear of the Lord is the beginning of wisdom" (Proverbs 9:10).

THE SIMPLICITY OF INTEGRITY

I often tell people that if they will learn to minimize the magnitude and frequency of their mistakes, their lives will be much, much simpler. Easier said than done? Well, sure, but there are some clear guidelines for handling a variety of mistakes that can cause anyone to compromise his or her integrity if not prepared in advance. Each one involves a willingness to face head-on some things that most people try to ignore. Amazingly, life will actually get easier if you don't dodge these sometimes painful realities:

1. Be willing to feel the fear of failure.
2. Be willing to face the conflict when others oppose you.
3. Be willing to endure criticism when you hold on to your dream.
4. Be willing to go through mental and emotional pain. (The closer you are to pain, the closer God is to making your dreams a reality.)

5. Be willing to be unconventional and try things outside the norm.

6. Be willing to accept the fact that many times dreams are birthed when mental, emotional, physical, and financial pain is at its greatest.

7. Be willing to stand up for things worth fighting for.

Point #7 is especially pertinent to issues in a person's private, family, and public worlds. Too many people are confused about what is worth a battle, an issue that author Patrick Morley addresses brilliantly in his classic book, *The Man in the Mirror*. He offers five suggestions about what to fight for:

1. Fight for a relationship, not against it.
2. Fight for reconciliation, not alienation.
3. Fight to preserve a friendship, not to destroy it.
4. Fight to save your marriage, not to cash in on it.
5. Fight to solve problems, not to create them.

THE PEACE OF CONFIDENT LIVING

Many folks have in their minds a false picture of a confident person. They imagine a bouncy, energetic, in-your-face man or woman who will speak his or her mind to the wall if no one else will listen. But the genuine picture of confidence is a person at peace. Peace comes to someone whose inner life is consistent with his or her outer life. The confident person exudes peace to those around.

Living with integrity also brings you peace with the Author of peace, God Almighty. Being at peace with God puts you at peace with yourself, your spouse, your children, and with most anyone else you encounter. When God is part of everything you do, you'll enjoy a quality of life that most people—no matter how successful—dream about but never experience.

What is peace of mind worth? Elvis Presley once said, "I would give a million dollars in cash to have peace of mind for just twenty-four hours." Elvis placed a pretty high price on peace, and well he should. I know I had to pay an extraordinary price for mine.

LIGHTS...CAMERAS...DISASTER

MY MOTION PICTURE STORY—PART 2

Since I didn't have money to pay the remaining post-production charges for Squezze Play, *I did the only thing I could think of: I begged MGM to send me a print anyway so we could hold our premiere as scheduled. A long 24 hours after my pleading phone call, MGM responded that, because my credit seemed good (and maybe because they were having mercy on a "first-timer"), they would send a print. Although I didn't feel like much of a champion, I had won in a must-win situation.*

The night Squezze Play *premiered, the Chateau Theater looked as if it belonged on Hollywood Boulevard instead of North Story Road in Irving, Texas. Red carpet stretched from the theater door to the curb while stretch limos deposited the football player stars in front of a fawning crowd. Inside was a movie mogul's dream—a packed house. Before the film rolled, an evangelist friend of mine offered an invocation—something I had promised God I would make sure we did in the event we actually had a world premiere. Then I introduced each of the Dallas Cowboys individually, and each shared his own reminiscences with the crowd. Best of all, the audience loved the picture. But our gala evening didn't end with the closing credits. The reception at the Texas Stadium Club overlooking the Cowboys' home field was nearly as spectacular as the movie showing itself. I rented the jumbo electronic scoreboard to pay tribute to all those who had brought the motion picture into being. Yet my investors made me feel as if I were the one who had made the whole experience possible. After meeting my wife Kay, several said she was beautiful enough to have been the leading lady.*

But good times, as they say, don't last forever. Mine barely lasted through the night of the premiere. I still hadn't paid for the movie print we showed, and my financial life plunged. Within two months of the Squezze Play *premiere, I was thrown into involuntary bankruptcy court by three people who had created our motion picture poster. And I only owed them $6,000—one-tenth of the MGM debt! What these folks really wanted was to frighten me enough so I would drop the movie in their laps and run.*

It didn't work. Instead, I sought protection from the federal court in Dallas. The day I was to appear in court, no one else was there. As I stood alone and perplexed in the halls of justice, an honorable-looking gentleman came out of a side room. While he removed what appeared to be a judge's robe, I ventured a question: "Excuse me, sir, would you be the honorable Judge John Ford?"

"Yes," he replied, "I am Judge Ford. What can I do for you?"

"Your honor, I am William Chaffin. I would like to discuss the motion picture Squezze Play *with you."*

"So you're the motion picture magnate I've heard so much about." The judge's eyes twinkled. "Come into my chamber, and let's visit regarding your problem."

Once in his private office, the judge sized me up quickly. "William, you're into a project far bigger than you are!" He went on to say he had checked me out and discovered I was a solid citizen in the community—a good family man, a person of integrity, a church-goer with a strong professional reputation, and a life member of the Dallas Chamber of Commerce.

After a 40-minute interview, Judge Ford concluded, "William Chaffin, I believe in you. I am going to give you a reasonable period of time to sell the assets of Squezze Play. *Don't try to get the motion picture in distribution. I want to keep things simple and to keep everything intact."*

I was deeply grateful for this good man's wisdom and mercy and promised to honor his trust to the best of my ability. For 20 months I was a "man with a mission." Several times I came close to selling the assets of Squezze Play—the movie print, music royalties, and ancillary rights—but the deals never quite came together. Although I was determined to make it happen, God had another idea.

Despite my best work, my life was out of control. I slept poorly, ate poorly, and gave up exercising. I lost 30 pounds I didn't need to lose, but just when I thought for sure I was on a "runaway freight train," a light appeared at the end of the tunnel.

Nearly out of the blue, five oil men—and over-the-top Cowboys fans—from Odessa, Texas, offered me $1.5 million cash for the movie. Judge Ford approved their offer, and we were to close and fund the sale in 45 days. I drank in the relief—until three days into the 45-day period. I received a foreclosure notice on my home, and that's when my serious trouble began, not because of the bank's action, but because I panicked.

Time for an observation on this story: The next time you see news of a high-profile person in trouble and you think to yourself, "In my right mind, I would never do that," you're quite correct. In your right mind, you wouldn't do it. But when you panic, you lose your rational mind. All you can think about is the terrifying "here and now." Any hopes about "down the road" don't even register.

On the jumbo screen in my mind, I saw my family evicted from our beautiful home—my wife, two children, three dogs, and all our furniture on the curb along our quiet neighborhood street. I watched our neighbors drive by wagging their heads, and in truth, there would be a lot for them to wag about. I was five months behind on our mortgage payments.

To dig myself out, I made an ill-advised quick turnaround deal to sell part of my interest as general partner and, executive producer. That, I calculated, would give me enough cash to cure the delinquent payments and keep the motion picture alive until the *final "big sale." My rationale went something like this: In 45 days, the federal court will disperse the $1.5 million, and my $300,000 worth of creditors will be made whole, dollar for dollar. The limited partners will get their money back, along with their share of the profits, the short-term investors will get their money, plus the return agreed upon, and I will get my share. In a month and a half we would all go our merry ways. It was a great theory, but in my panic, I had neglected to explain to the quick-turn investors how I expected the deal to play out.*

One of my new investors—an attorney—heard on the street (the worst possible way to find out!) that I was in involuntary bankruptcy. He checked into the court docket, and, sure enough, Sunshine Films, Squezze Play, *and William Chaffin were featured players. He and the other nine people to whom I had sold my interest immediately filed fraud charges with the district attorney's office. Then, in the things-going-from-bad-to-worse department, the DA secured an indictment for fraud and securities violation from a grand jury. Suddenly I was one of those people "you read about." Three-fourths of page one in the* Dallas Times Herald *and* Dallas Morning News *business sections announced my problems under the headline "Baptist Deacon Bilks Investors." Not exactly the good witness I had always hoped to be. And not exactly the news my Odessa investors wanted to see.*

They read the sensationalized article and were spooked. The broker handling their transaction called to say they wanted out of the deal. They would not be signing a contract, nor cutting an escrow check to the federal court. When I got that news, I was devastated. The Odessa group had been my last hope to salvage the motion picture and, so I thought, my life. I pulled into a shopping center parking lot, slumped over the steering wheel, and cried like a baby.

BILL'S HARD LESSON #2

MAINTAIN CONTROL OF YOUR LIFE BY NOT RISKING YOUR MONEY OR REPUTATION ON SOMETHING YOU KNOW NOTHING ABOUT.

Chapter 3

THE HOPE OF INTEGRITY

Few things are more explosive than an idea whose "hour has come," and in business, money flows to good ideas. An entrepreneur knows that if funding dries up, his or her business concept needs an upgrade to get investment dollars flowing again. In fact, every major accomplishment in American history has resulted from a dream, a vision, or some far-fetched idea, driven by people of character who are relentlessly dedicated to making life better.

SMALL STARTS, BIG HOPES

We all know Alexander Graham Bell invented the telephone in 1876, but by communications standards today, his first accomplishment was not very impressive. He conveyed a one-way phone call eight miles. How much commerce would we do now if we could make only one-way phone calls over a distance of less than ten miles? Bell's original idea needed others to come along and build on what he started. If Mr. Bell appeared on the scene today, he would likely be awestruck by the advancement in telecommunications. Unfortunately, people regularly minimize an original idea that doesn't seem significant at the time. But progress is like a relay race. One inventor passes the baton to another, upgrading the original invention each step of the way.

The Wright Brothers offer another instructive illustration. Orville and Wilbur Wright achieved the first-ever powered airplane flight. Yet their wood, wire, and cloth craft flew just 120 feet. On a football field, that would be like taking off at your goal and flying to your own 40-yard line—but their far-fetched idea did get off the ground! Since then, inventors, engineers, and pilots have given us the airpower to fight wars, commercial jets to convey passengers, cargo planes for freight, packages, and the mail, and—perhaps most remarkable of all—the space shuttle.

But what is the fuel behind these accomplishments built on ideas that seem so outlandish? The energy source is hope. Hope can literally keep people alive, and it drives the conviction people need to accomplish great things.

After the Twin Towers went down on 9/11, I was amazed at how many people hunkered down in crisis and survival mode. I saw this time and again at my speaking engagements in the weeks and months after that terrible day. No matter to whom I was speaking—corporations, schools, city governments, churches, athletic teams, kids at risk, parents, or prison inmates—I determined to be a proponent of what I call a "fresh and vibrant vision of the future full of hope."

"That's great," you may be saying at this point, "but how do hope and integrity fit together?"

I'm glad you asked.

THE HOPE CONNECTION

Hope needs assurance that it will be fulfilled, and assurance comes from walking with integrity. It can be the integrity of deeply believing the rightness of your idea (no matter how peculiar it seems to others). And it most assuredly grows out of knowing for sure that "you're doing the right thing," no matter what others may be up to. The conviction of having God's favor because you're walking in accord with His values stirs hope daily in the people who live His way.

People become hopeless because they hope in the wrong things. They cast about for something visible, tangible, or material on which to pin their hopes—real estate, precious metals, stocks, bonds, positions of power, prestige, or popularity—then suffer when it fails them, as it inevitably does.

Hope in hopeless things can be terrifying. When such hope fails, it leaves frustration, brokenness, and cavernous regret. Even when this kind of hope is fulfilled, it is often worse than failure since the thing hoped for always turns out to be hollow. Whether satisfied or not, hoping in what is hopeless breeds loneliness, emptiness, alcoholism, health problems, divorce, and often suicide.

Hope that grows from a life of integrity, on the other hand, is anything but hopeless. You'll notice that in the Bible, hope is a noun, not a verb. That means it's something we possess, not something we do. Hope is a gift from God, resulting from living with integrity. Jeremiah 29:11 explains how this comes straight from the heart of God: "'I know the plans I have for you'—this is the Lord's declaration—'plans for your welfare, not for disaster, to give you a future and a hope'" (HCSB). God offers people hope that is the fulfillment of everything the human heart longs for: justice, peace, freedom, human rights, no sorrow, no tears, no pain, no war, no death. God promises all that and infinitely more, and it can all start right here and now as you walk with God in integrity.

A person of character stays the course, never wavering, never giving up hope, never compromising the integrity of his or her cause. Strangely, not everyone gets this connection. Former Georgia Tech coach George O'Leary didn't think integrity and character had much value. After his stint with the Georgia team, Notre Dame hired him to be their head football coach, but the school fired O'Leary after only five days on the job. His transgression? Résumé fraud. O'Leary claimed to have a master's degree he didn't have, and the accolades he boasted for his accomplishments as a college football player were a lie. The reason for Coach O'Leary's disconnect is obvious in the comment he shared with a reporter who interviewed him the day he was dismissed. "Coach O'Leary," the reporter asked, "where does integrity enter the picture for what you do?" To which O'Leary responded, "What does integrity have to do with playing football on a hundred-yard field?"

Excuse me? Obviously, the Tech coach had never talked to John Wooden about the influence of integrity and character on winning big.

Such integrity gaps happen in the corporate world as well as in big league sports. In Fort Worth, Texas, Dave Edmondson, the CEO of Radio Shack, was being groomed to take over as chairman of the board. Only months before the transition, the board of directors stunned the company and business pundits by asking for Mr. Edmondson's resignation. What did they know that the rest of us didn't? Résumé fraud again. Edmondson claimed to have earned degrees in theology and psychology, but neither had ever happened. In a somewhat disconcerting case of "mixed messages," though, the board gave Mr. Edmondson a $1.5 million severance package. It almost makes lying seem profitable, and I admit I'm still struggling with that one! It's amazing someone could go so wrong but end up seeming so right.

THE INTEGRITY SAFETY NET

If you've ever watched the high-wire act at a circus, you've noticed that, no matter how expert the performers, there's usually a safety net between them and the ground. Even though the performers are so good there's almost no possibility of their falling, the consequences of a fall would be too tragic to take chances. They hope not to fall, of course, but have provided a "safe passage" if they do.

Living a life of integrity needs a similar precaution, and the safety net for protecting integrity is a person's ethics. If you've structured your "performance" in life around a set of standards for your behavior, you will have something to catch you if you are tempted to stumble along the way.

Ethics is a vital part of the integrity and character picture. High ethical standards help you live mindfully, to take care how you act, and even about how you feel. It isn't enough to follow your feelings or fly by instinct when you ponder what to do or how to live. There is a significant difference between your ethical standards and your "feelings" about what is right or not.

If ethics were just a matter of feelings, then nothing could be said to be wrong with prejudices. It would be "ethical" to discriminate against people you don't like. Feelings might say yes, but ethics say no. Ethics stand outside of your own subjective reality. While feelings are easily manipulated, standards are not. Ethics provide the tools for thinking about difficult matters. Struggle and uncertainty are part of living ethically since taking a stand can be quite hard at times. But holding to ethical standards does make it easier to do the right thing every time. Without ethics to live by, consistently doing the right thing is nearly impossible.

Embracing integrity and character as part of one's lifestyle makes life intriguing, often beautiful, and always full of possibilities and promise. It also produces some wonderful by-products.

ETHICS BRINGS INTEGRITY BRINGS HOPE BRINGS...RESULTS!

A winning lifestyle is always the result of living a high standard you impose on yourself. I have a keynote address called "Get Your Head in the Game" in which I point out that showing up physically and being on the job every day is important, but showing up mentally is even more critical. In sports and in business, mental errors can be very costly. That's what once cost an otherwise stellar pro basketball team a legitimate shot at the championship.

The Dallas Mavericks, a #1 seed in the 2007 NBA playoffs, lost to a #8 seed in a seven-game series. Never before in NBA history had a #1 team lost to such a low-ranked team. The Maverick players were there physically, but no one showed up mentally. They played lackluster basketball—without intensity and lacking focus. They showed no enthusiasm, no passion. (Pardon my bluntness, but as a long-time observer of basketball—Basketball Bill, right?—and fan of the Mavericks, I couldn't help but notice this.) When there was a loose ball or a long rebound, they just stood around like a bunch of guys with their hands in their pockets. In my opinion, they embarrassed themselves, the ownership, the fans, and the city of Dallas—this from a team that had won 67 games during the regular season. When playoff time comes, though, everyone is back to the starting line, and everyone better show up—mentally as well as physically!

In business, getting your head in the game begins—like everything else in the corporation—with the folks at the top. One company I worked with had a marvelous view of the organization's leadership. The company maintained: "the one thing that we could lose that would drive us out of business most readily would be our inspired leadership." Wow! Inspired leadership—men and women in charge who are dedicated to standards worth standing up for. High costs can be overcome by increasing the degree of perfection with which each part of the job is done. Service failures can be overcome by improving customer-oriented service. Improved handling of labor problems can be learned, methods improved. But the one thing that cannot be overcome is the loss of inspired leaders. Being "inspired" means not doing anything half-heartedly. You cannot be casually involved. You must be totally committed. When a leader seeks to re-create in others the strong core values he or she embraces, that example and role model will be multiplied many times over.

Leaders too often mistake efficiency for effectiveness, but the two are not synonymous. Let me explain (with another Texas sports story).

In the early 1960s the Dallas Cowboys were highly efficient at moving the football up and down the field between the two 20-yard lines. However, when they got inside the 20 (the "red zone") the team often couldn't get across the goal line or even score a field goal. Their efficiency of play didn't make them effective at winning—until it came together on one critical afternoon. An NFC playoff game between the Cowboys and the Cleveland Browns on December 24, 1967, marked a turning point at which the team shed its label of not being able to win the "big game." The final score was an impressive 52 to 14 over the Browns, and it moved the Cowboys to a new plateau. After that, under Coach Tom Landry's (inspired) leadership, the Dallas Cowboys made the playoffs more than 15 times during the next three decades. They had transformed the efficiency of their play into the effectiveness of putting points on the scoreboard.

An inspired leader will never be accused of ordering people around or "slave-driving" them. Instead, that individual will inspire others to drive themselves toward a common goal. A good leader hires the entire person with all their strengths and flaws and develops the strengths. If you do that, you will not only build a good employee but a bigger person as well. I discovered, though, in a harder way than I would have ever hoped, that becoming a "bigger person" can be pretty tough.

LIGHTS...CAMERAS...DISASTER

MY MOTION PICTURE STORY—PART 3

The media tried me four months before my trial opened in the courtroom. And since I was out of money long before my case came up, the court appointed my attorney. The truth is, I had so little money, paying the lawyer would have been the least of my concerns. I wondered from day to day how to put food on the table.

In October, our financial desperation forced Kay to wonder out loud, "Honey, don't you have a friend who's the general manager of the Loew's Anatole Hotel?" (She knew that I did.) "Would you humble yourself, and go ask Mark for a job as a bellman so we can have a little Christmas money for our family?"

Even though I was typically spending the first five hours of every day preparing for trial with my lawyer, the next morning, I dressed in a three-piece suit to go see Mark. Since I arrived at his office without an appointment, I was relieved to find him there. He graciously ushered me in.

"Billy Boy," he said, "you're looking sharp. What brings you here today?"

"I'm applying for a job," I answered.

Mark grinned. "You must be living a charmed life. Our director of catering and banquet services just got promoted to a new position, and with your people and communication skills, and your sales background, you'd be a perfect fit to replace him."

Mark relaxed, leaning back in his plush chair. He propped his feet up on his desk, probably feeling as if I'd just solved a big problem for him in his catering department. Unfortunately I didn't let his relief last long.

"My friend, I appreciate your vote of confidence, but that's not the position I am interested in. In good conscience, I cannot take that job. In two months I will be going on trial for my freedom because of the motion picture Squezze Play. *Mark, I want to wear the green uniform of a bellman, taking care of your hotel guests."*

The hotel manager just about fell out of his chair, but he was touched by my candor and humility. Without comment, he called the personnel office and said he wanted me processed, with clothes issued and tailored, and on the floor in three days.

I was assigned the late afternoon and evening shift—3 o'clock until midnight. On my first day, I wondered how long it would be before someone I knew discovered me at the Anatole and asked, "Chaffin, what are you doing here as a bellman?" My stock answer was going to be, "I am providing a Christmas for my family."

Midway through my first shift, it was Charles Pistor, Chairman of the Board of Republic National Bank, the second largest bank in the Southwest, who showed up. "Hi, Bill, my wife and I have a couple with us from out of state, and we just got turned away from the French restaurant. The maitre`d said they were booked for the rest of the night. Here is thirty dollars if you can get us a table for four."

I went to the maitre'd and told him I had some good friends hosting out of state guests that really needed a table. He had been holding one back and said, "The table is yours." I split the thirty dollars with my new friend, the maitre'd. And my old friend Charles Pistor was grateful I had salvaged his evening. How ironic, I mused, a lowly bellman helping a top business executive with something he desperately wanted. Maybe this position has more value than I thought.

A few evenings later, a distinguished-looking gentleman with a lordly accent arrived from England. I gave him my typical "positively outrageous service," and when we arrived at his suite, he handed me a welcome bit of cash.

"Bill, here's a tip for your regular service. In addition, I have a special request. Here are two hundred dollar bills if you find me a hot woman for the night."

Stifling my shock, I responded, "Sir, that is not part of my job description."

"You must have a serious eye problem...I am flashing two Ben Franklins in front of you."

"No, sir, my eyes are just fine. Perhaps you have a hearing problem because I have already given you my answer—a resounding 'no'."

Although as I left his suite, the man was shaking his head in disbelief, that moment provided one of my great lessons in integrity. At the time, $200 would have made a big difference in my quality of life, but I had a long-established personal standard that "I'm not for sale." And I believe God honored my choice to do the right thing in the face of a significant temptation. Overall that evening, I made $264 in tips—the biggest payday of my entire two months as a bellman!

Kay and I eeked out a Christmas for our kids, and then, with my bellman's job behind me, the trial for my freedom began on January 20, 1982. I took the witness stand to explain how I had tried to keep the motion picture project alive, and a strong line-up of character witnesses supported me, including Cowboys superstar Drew Pearson. It helped, too, that an audit showed appropriate accountability for every dollar of my $530,000 budget.

The trial was an unspeakable emotional and mental roller-coaster. After a week of reliving the heartache of the spoiled movie venture, my sentencing was to come down on January 28, 1982. That day, Kay packed a sack lunch for me in which she had scribbled a love note: "Sweetheart, I believe in you and love you unconditionally, and whatever happens today, whether you get probation or a prison sentence, I will be by your side all the way."

The note, of course, was the best part of my lunch, feeding both my empty heart and soul. It renewed my hope that I would survive no matter what life lessons I would have to face—or where.

The jury foreman handed the verdict to Judge John Ovard, and in the stifling silence of the courtroom, the judge ordered me to stand. "William Chaffin, you have hereby been sentenced to ten years in prison and a twelve-thousand-five-hundred dollar fine."

I was stunned. That was the maximum possible sentence for a first-time offense! (My brother John later heard that the jury thought I showed no remorse, and that's why they gave me such a severe penalty.) Kay began hyperventilating, and a physician friend came to her aid. Someone handed me my Criswell Study Bible *as I was hustled from the courtroom. Kay and I blew our final kisses to each another.*

The bailiff kindly asked if I would like a cell by myself for one hour. With tears streaming down my cheeks, I choked, "Sir, I would appreciate that very much."

What followed is what I call my darkest hour on Planet Earth— in three, distinct 20-minute segments. For the first 20 minutes, I experienced a "spiritual freefall." It seemed as if I were tumbling though space, out of control, isolated from God, family, friends— even my enemies. Never before or since, have I felt so helpless or hopeless. My inner voice taunted, "Bill Chaffin, your life is history. There is no future for you. You are a casualty on the battlefield of life." I slumped against the wall in that cell and cried out loud, "God Almighty, is this it? Have I come to the end of the road?"

During the second 20 minutes, I fussed at God and complained that my adversaries had wrongly stripped me of what I had worked for. "Dear God," I lamented, "the people who took me to trial have been ruthless towards me and my family. The bitterness, the hateful spirit, and the ugly feelings I have towards them is something that You, Lord, are going to have to help me work through."

Incredibly, at that instant, something that felt like a bolt of lightning zapped me with a new attitude and a new heart, and I forgave them all. God showed me I was the one at fault. I had "blown it." And in the next incredible instant, I accepted 100% of the blame for my mistake. It was a critical step in coming clean before God and others, and it began an arduous process of breaking down my cocky, defensive, and arrogant spirit.

In the third 20 minutes, God gave me my "marching orders." I knew I was going to be living in Satan's den for a long time (although I hoped not the full ten years). I felt God say to me, "William, while you're living in this forsaken place, I want you to do the following: where there is hatred, I want you to sow love, where there is injury, pardon, where there is despair, hope, where there is darkness, light, where there is sadness, joy, and where there is conflict, I want you to be an instrument of My peace."

With that message stirring my heart, I greeted two guards who arrived to "book me in." And what a humiliating process! They took my fingerprints, a classic set of two mug shots, battered me with questions, and marched me to a dressing area, where they ordered me to undress and take a shower. As I toweled down after the shower, three guards approached with a monstrous tank of foul-smelling liquid.

"Gentlemen," I asked, "what's in that container?"

"A chemical that kills lice and other parasites many inmates bring in off the street. Everyone gets the treatment—no exceptions." With that, they sprayed me from head to toe.

As I was standing there naked and dripping with putrid oil, one of the guards added quietly, "There's something else you have that we need."

"Now what could that be?" I stared at the man. "I have been stripped of my dignity, honor, self-worth, family, friends, reputation, money, career, freedom—and my clothes! What could possibly be left?"

"Your wedding ring. Is it 14-karat gold?"

Another piece of my heart died inside. "Yes. Of course."

"An expensive ring with diamonds will be irresistible to other inmates," explained a guard. "If you insist on going to sleep tonight with your wedding ring on, your cellmates will remove the ring from your finger. If they can't slip it off, they will cut your finger off at the base with a homemade shank and take the ring. It's amazing how much mileage they can get bartering with something of that value."

I could see the man was serious. He genuinely had my best interest in mind. As I wrestled the ring off my finger, the guard's alternative scenario made me shudder. "Please put my ring in safe-keeping until I get out."

Placing my wedding band in the guard's outstretched hand, I thought, "I cannot believe this is happening to me." It was as near to an out-of-body experience as I've ever had.

I dressed in my new prison clothes and thought of the fine suit I had worn just a few months ago to my interview with Mark at the Loew's Anatole Hotel as I headed to my new accommodations—the "tank." The tank offered six cells with eight bunks per cell. Each iron-barred room was only thirteen feet long and nine feet wide. Living on the system's terms was going to be a major adjustment on my part. (How would you like to have seven other people sleeping in your bedroom?)

I checked out my surroundings: one telephone and one shower (with a perpetually stopped up drain) for 48 inmates, three toilets, one sink with a mirror, and one television. Four dozen men shared less floor space than the presidential suite at the Anatole!

There were metal tables where I could write my diary notes, but the same tables were used for meals. There was no privacy; everything was out in the open. The tank's spokesman, elected by the inmates, ruled as the arbitrator and mediator on all issues between inmates and guards alike.

My wardrobe consisted of two white prison coveralls, two pairs of socks, two undershorts, and a pair of plastic open-toed slippers. Perhaps the worst part, though, was the food. I would have expected better meals in a refugee camp: A hard-boiled egg and one piece of white bread for breakfast, turnip greens and some other overcooked stuff for lunch, and more of the same at dinner. I lost 23 pounds in my first 30 days of incarceration. It's a very effective diet if you need to lose weight (which I didn't), so between my environment and the poor food, I did the only thing any normal person would. I got deathly sick.

BILL'S HARD LESSON #3

WHEN YOU MAKE A MISTAKE, BURY YOUR PRIDE AND TAKE THE BLAME.

Chapter 4

INTEGRITY-DRIVEN

It's been said a person's true character shows by what he or she does "alone in the dark." While that may be true enough, I've observed a way to determine in broad daylight what a person's character is made of. You can tell a great deal about yourself and other people if you pay attention to one particular thing most adults do over and over.

I've been a licensed driver for more than half a century, and after putting in thousands of miles behind the wheel, I've come to a remarkable conclusion about people in their cars: You are how you drive. That's such a revealing truth, it's worth spending a chapter exploring this one deep-seated indicator of a man's or woman's character.

Next time you're on the road, pick out a car to watch. In fact, if you want to do an in-depth experiment to understand what I'm talking about, choose a car to follow, and stay with him or her for at least 15 minutes (this works best if you can spend time on the open road as well as going through three to four miles of traffic lights). Let's talk about what you might see and what it means. You'll discover a lot about that person even though the two of you have never met.

THE TEN RULES OF THE ROAD—AND CHARACTER

1) DARTING IN AND OUT OF TRAFFIC REVEALS AN IMPULSIVE AND CONTROLLING SPIRIT.

"Darting" is a sudden, swift movement, without any advance warning and usually without advance planning on the part of the driver. It's an abrupt, impulsive act. To be impulsive is to be moved by seemingly involuntary reactions. The impulsive person's mental and emotional state is unstable. Anything goes. "If it feels good do it" is the attitude of this unpredictable individual. In Chapter 2, I pointed out that before you can act right you must be thinking right, but a person who drives erratically demonstrates an impatient and cluttered mind. He or she can't wait to get to the next open spot in traffic and doesn't care about endangering others to do it. Yet this abrupt action is not even part of some great plan. Once he or she gets to that next spot, the only plan this person has is to swing into the next place just to get there, too. Undisciplined and out of control, the darter is on the way to a "messed up" life. He or she will zip in front of someone else once too often or misjudge how much room there is between two cars and bring disaster upon everyone around.

2) RUNNING A YELLOW LIGHT JUST AS IT'S TURNING RED REPRESENTS LIVING ON THE RAGGED EDGE.

This person throws caution to the wind with an attitude that says, "Here I come. You'd better get out of my way because I'm in a hurry." This pattern spills over into every part of this individual's life. Running the light reflects moving forward without restraint, with no regard for anyone else. Like playing "chicken" or "Russian Roulette," the wilder the better. People like this feel as if they're in control of life (theirs and everyone else's), but that's merely an illusion. They're really playing a game of chance in which no one is in control, and everyone they meet is at risk. The kind of catastrophic potential in this person is why your state's driver's manual likely labels an intersection the most dangerous spot on any road.

3) RIDING THE BUMPER OF THE PERSON IN FRONT OF YOU IS INTIMIDATION IN THE EXTREME.

A driver who follows too close wants to force his or her will on others. This version of the I'll-get-what-I-want attitude threatens, "If you don't move to another lane, I'm going to run over you." Causing fear in another person is this individual's way of getting his or her way. At home, someone like this manipulates and stifles other family members. Dominating and tyrannizing gives great satisfaction to this jerk. And broken relationships are the inevitable result of such losing behavior.

4) GOING 10 TO 15 MILES PER HOUR OVER THE SPEED LIMIT DENOTES ALWAYS TRYING TO BEAT THE SYSTEM.

Speeders think they don't have to play by the rules. Like people who run traffic lights, these folks are deluded in thinking they're in control. The reality is that when speeding, no one can "stop on a dime." There's also an illusion that speeding makes a significant difference in how soon you arrive at your destination. Around town, a few miles per hour faster will net you only a few measly seconds on your trip. In Texas, if you cause an accident in which someone is killed and the law can prove you were speeding, your "negligent homicide" conviction could get you up to 25 years in prison—pretty high stakes for trying to get somewhere a few seconds sooner than anyone else. This is a rude awakening for people who think they're in charge of life but actually are completely out of control. I never cease to be amazed at how many people act like they live in a world in which borders, barriers, and limits don't matter!

5) COMING TO A ROLLING STOP AT A STOP SIGN INDICATES REBELLION AGAINST BOUNDARIES.

When you see this happen, the person behind the wheel is stretching the boundaries of the law, justifying in his or her mind why coming to a complete stop isn't necessary (after all, there was no traffic in sight no one was close enough to be a threat etc.). But my state's driving manual directs, "Come to a complete stop for two full seconds, look both ways to make sure it's safe, and then proceed." No exceptions. Just stop. People who don't stop have a life theme of, "Don't confuse me with the facts; my mind is already made up." They pigishly ignore the reality that boundaries are established for the best interests of everyone and that the constraints don't benefit us if no one takes them seriously. Too many people in our society don't want limits, but this sort of unrestrained behavior is, at best, irresponsible and, at worst, shows that the person is willing to die (and take others along) just for the selfish personal "freedom" he thinks is his right. But it doesn't work at a stop sign, and it doesn't work in life.

6) NOT LETTING SOMEONE CHANGE LANES IN FRONT OF YOU IS BULLISH AND SELFISH.

No matter how big a hurry you're in, being thoughtful enough to make room for someone else will never cost you significant time. Selfishness characterizes this person's concern for his or her own interest and demonstrates a zero regard for anybody else. Anyone this self-serving needs a dose of caring about what is happening around him or her. Like it or not, we live in this world with a lot of other people, and we are all better off finding the win-win in any situation. Allowing someone to move into the lane not only helps the other person but keeps traffic moving smoothly. Being rude is not cool—it is ill-mannered and uncultured. The Golden Rule applies: Treat others as you would like to be treated.

7) A LACK OF COMMON COURTESY ON THE OPEN ROAD DEMONSTRATES THAT YOU REALLY DON'T CARE FOR OR HONOR OTHER PEOPLE.

Without courtesy to other drivers, a person reflects a belief that "it's all about me." The word "honor" means to esteem, to respect, and to dignify another person. Doing what is morally right demonstrates honor. When someone has a healthy awareness of his effect on others, he or she will show good manners and polite consideration of everyone else.

8) NEGLIGENT DRIVING REVEALS THAT A PERSON IS A FOOLISH RISK TAKER.

Carelessness may give this person an adrenalin rush, but it doesn't change the fact that he or she is stupidly indifferent to potential harm. Any time someone takes a risk—whether in business or any other pursuit—there is a chance of loss, but the reasonable approach to risk is to make sure the potential benefit outweighs the risk. Yet this calculation is never part of the equation for a risky driver. His or her emotional satisfaction is all that matters. This individual is oblivious to the possibility of hurting others, and this losing behavior needlessly exposes innocent people to life-changing peril.

9) DON'T HANG AROUND A CAR THAT IS SERIOUSLY DENTED—IT REPRESENTS SOMEONE WHO IS CARELESS.

There is also a strong possibility that this car is uninsured, so you can add "irresponsible" to the character flaws here. The person takes little pride in what he or she has and is reckless and thoughtless. Sloppy and unorganized, this individual has a severely deficient sense of value. You'll find that someone like this cannot respect others because he or she doesn't have a healthy self-respect.

10) DISTRACTED DRIVING MEANS THE DRIVER HAS LOST FOCUS ON THE RIGHT PRIORITIES.

Highway studies tell us that 55% of all accidents are caused by distractions. The scene in front of you can change dramatically in even just the one or two seconds you take your eyes off the road to change a CD, reach for a soft drink, write yourself a note, pick up something you dropped, make a cell phone call, put on make-up, or adjust your tie knot. Way too often, as the stats suggest, serious bodily injury or loss of life is the consequence. People who let distractions hinder their driving operate in their own worlds, losing sight of what is really important at the moment. They disregard the danger their actions cause other people.

In 1990's winsome Academy Award Best Picture, Jessica Tandy plays "Miss Daisy," a well-to-do elderly southern woman who causes one too many driving mishaps. As a result, her son

(Dan Aykroyd) permanently suspends the elder woman's driving privileges and hires Hoke Colburn (Morgan Freeman) to see that "momma" gets safely wherever she wants to go.

Angry at first over her son's "insensitivity," Daisy eventually settles into her new life around town with a chauffeur whose impeccable driving abilities are clearly the outer evidence of a deep and well-ordered inner life. *Driving Miss Daisy*'s Hoke Colburn represents what I would wish for anyone reading this book—to be a flawless driver. Why? Because when you get behind the wheel of a car, the integrity of your character goes on display for the world to see. If you live with integrity, you'll drive with integrity.

LIGHTS...CAMERAS...DISASTER

MY MOTION PICTURE STORY—PART 4

I was sick enough to be moved to another tank—the flu tank. The surroundings were as dismal as I felt, and after a week there, at least the regular tank didn't seem quite so bad.

Part of life "inside" is that a guard escorts prisoners everywhere they go, and the one who accompanied me back to my living quarters noticed something that changed my prison life for good. "Chaffin, I'm looking at your buff-card and from what I can tell, you don't look like a convict."

"Thank you, sir," I said. "I made a big mistake that I'm paying a high price for."

He wondered, "Can you type?"

"No, sir—but I can cook. In fact, I cooked in the United States Army for two years."

My escort brightened. "Boy, do we need you in the kitchen."

The process of confirming an inmate as a trusty (prison jargon—and spelling!—for a prisoner with higher-than-average duties and responsibilities) normally took ten days, but in 90 minutes, I had my trusty uniform and was ushered into the kitchen. Sgt. Hebner, the correctional officer in charge there, could have been a Marine drill sergeant—crew cut, stocky build, a powerful, harsh voice.

Hebner greeted me with a roar, "Chaffin, what do you know about cooking?"

"Sir, before I tell you what I know about cooking, please tell me about your kitchen operation—what you're feeding the inmate population and what you're feeding the officers and guards."

I had noticed from the first days of my confinement that many correctional personnel were overweight from eating a lot of starchy foods, so I offered to make 30 individual salads and some homemade salad dressing. Glad to encourage any improvement, Hebner accepted my list of fresh veggies, and the supervisor-turned-supply-officer quickly provided lettuce, shredded carrots, celery, tomatoes, radishes, bell pepper, onions, and eggs for hard-boiling. The next day for lunch, the 30 colorful salads "went like hotcakes."

Sgt. Hebner marveled at my success. "Chaffin, we're onto something special. You made me look real good. Where do we go from here?" And the Dallas County Jail salad bar was born. (No matter what the environment, better ideas are always welcome.)

Hebner also explained to me that a new $2 million stainless steel kitchen was due to open in three weeks on the ninth floor of the Dallas County Jail. So I laid out menu plans for the new kitchen. I promised Sgt. Hebner omelets, eggs any style, bacon, sausage, ham, French toast, Belgian waffles, pancakes, and fresh oranges sliced on a bed of lettuce for breakfast for the officers and guards, and he gave me carte blanche to order all the food I needed to plan menus for opening week. Hebner instructed all kitchen trustys to take orders from me. As my "pay," he allowed me to eat as well as the top jail commander, Captain Baker. It seemed too good to be true—behind bars and eating like a king. To acknowledge the whole kitchen crew, I also provided my workers the same royal diet.

Although abundant in privileges, my kitchen responsibilities also entailed the hardest work schedule I'd ever managed. I was up and in the kitchen every morning by 2:30 to start breakfast for 900 inmates. The grill in the new kitchen could have been in one of Dallas's finest restaurants, and it almost made scrambling a hundred dozen eggs fun. My team piled food into individual trays, loaded the meals onto carts, and rolled them to their respective floors. With inmates fed, by 5:30 I was preparing a gourmet breakfast for the officer's dining room. Once the dining room closed at 6:30, I fixed breakfast for the 20 kitchen helpers.

But the day had just begun. After all breakfasts were served, the pressure was on to have Jell-O and ten fancy salads for the officers' lunch, prepared and set up on the food line by 10:30. One especially bad-tempered guard who walked with a limp from being shot in the hip by an inmate warned that if I was ever late, by even one minute, he would bust me as a trusty. In truth what bugged him was that I was eating as well as the jail commander.

God gave me a passion to be the best trusty ever in the Dallas County Jail. That vision fueled my attitude and lifted my spirit. Every inmate battles his own "identity crisis" daily. Wearing white coveralls with "prisoner" on the back and a plastic wristband with a number but no name is desperately dehumanizing. What's worse, detention guards rank low on the government's pay scale, so they take out their frustrations on inmates by reminding prisoners over and over that, as felons and convicts, they're even lower than the guards. Some inmates crack under the pressure and go "off the wall," screaming obscenities at the guards. If confrontations turn to violence, an inmate ends up in solitary confinement—"the hole"—where living conditions are horrendous.

To keep my sanity, I turned to Scripture for counsel. James 1:19 gave me the edge in handling people in authority who tried to mess with my mind: "Be quick to hear, slow to speak, and slow to anger." The tongue is one of the smallest parts of the human body, but it can *get a person into trouble quicker than most anything else—whether you're in the "free world" or locked up in jail.*

Two months into my incarceration, thoughts of Kay and my children began to weigh heavily on my mind. Would they survive financially until I regained my freedom? I felt so badly about what I was dragging them through that I didn't even want Chad, age 12, and Noelle, age 8, to visit me. One Thursday evening on the phone, though, Kay brought me up short. "Your daughter would like to speak with you."

With that, she put Noelle on the phone. "Hi, Daddy. I miss you and love you a lot. Every day at school before I go to the playground I sit on a bench and pray for you. I pray that no one beats you up, that you have enough food to eat, and that you have a pillow under your head at night when you sleep. You call me 'daddy's little angel,' but you don't let me come see you. Please, can I come with Mommy and see you tomorrow night?"

Noelle's request confronted me with my own self-centeredness. Not wanting to see my children was about my pride, not about their needs. "Yes, little darling. Of course you can come. I can hardly wait to see you and Chad and Mommy."

Friday night visitation lasted from 7:00 to 9:00. When the intercom sputtered that my visitors had arrived, a baffling mixture of emotions welled up in me. While I was excited to see my family together, I was ashamed of what I had done to them. I also looked terrible. Having dropped from 200 to 170 pounds in just a month, my face was sunken and my skin colorless.

A guard escorted Kay, Noelle, and Chad to my living quarters where we talked on telephones while looking through a tiny glass window. "Daddy, thank you for letting me come visit you," Noelle chattered. "Step back so I can see you from head to toe." She told me I looked skinny, so I assured her that now that I had become a kitchen trusty, I would quickly regain the weight I had lost.

Then it was Chad's turn. He gave me a golden lesson in the value of making right choices, for on that crucial Friday night, he reminded me of something I'd done six years before. Only six years old at the time, Chad asked me one night to go with him to a roller skating party the next day, so I could teach him to skate. He didn't want to be embarrassed in front of the other boys. At first I said "no." I had tickets to go that Saturday afternoon with four clients to what would likely be the game that would send my Dallas Cowboys to the Super Bowl. Quickly realizing that Chad was heartbroken and afraid to face his buddies at the rink, I relented, gave away the tickets, and joined my son for a joyful afternoon of roller skating.

That night in the tank, Chad looked me in the eye through the prison visitor's window and asked, "Dad, remember that roller skating birthday party I went to in the first grade?"

"Yes, son, I remember."

"You gave up something special to go with me and teach me how to skate. I will never forget that. Now you are going through a dark hour. Dad, I believe in you. I forgive you, I love you, and I want you to know that you will have my full support while you are locked up. That's a promise."

With that, my tear ducts lost it. I've never been more thankful for one small choice. The investment paid off when I needed it most.

Through the tiny window, I gave my children a tour of my living quarters by pointing to my bunk, the telephone, and the table where I wrote my diary notes. To conclude our family time, we prayed together, and tears flowed again as I said goodbye. Noelle laid her little hand on the window, and I pressed my hand against hers on my side. That act said we were still a father-daughter team.

From that time on, the kids came to see me every Friday night. The guards noticed our closeness despite our separation and commented often about my beautiful family and how nicely dressed they were. But I couldn't imagine how I would survive without them for so long.

BILL'S HARD LESSON #4

KEEP YOUR PRIORITIES FOCUSED—NEVER UNDERESTIMATE THE VALUE OF MAKING GOOD CHOICES TODAY THAT WILL YIELD RICH DIVIDENDS IN THE LONG RUN.

Chapter 5

THE ATTITUDE OF
INTEGRITY

When I lost my trial, "the system" took everything from me—my freedom, dignity, honor, self-worth, family, friends, money, career, reputation, and even my clothes. But one thing nobody could strip from me was a good attitude. My attitude was my choice!

You may have heard before that your attitude is a choice, but you may not have realized what a crucial role attitude plays in living a life of integrity. We've discussed how the inner work of integrity is determined by your thought life and that your character determines what comes out in the way you live. Yet attitude is the crowning touch on a life of integrity. Attitude reflects to other people how you feel about life itself. And a person of impeccable integrity treasures life.

Herb Kelleher, founder of Southwest Airlines, sets the bar high in taking on new employees: "There is only one thing we are going to hire at Southwest Airlines, and that is called attitude. We can teach our people everything else we want them to know."

Mr. Kelleher understands that attitude is the basis of what comes out in a person's work. It is more fundamental than intelligence, talent, skills, and abilities. It will take you further than education, degrees, knowledge, and experience. And it will win you more true friends than personality, charisma, and appearance. When you have a positive, upbeat attitude, people love to be around you. They can't get enough of you—partly because a good attitude is so rare these days.

TEN TRUTHS OF ATTITUDE

You want to be different? Try having a good attitude, and you'll wear well with others. Your good attitude demonstrates the integrity of your heart. If you're right on the inside, your attitude will let it show on the outside.

Having a good attitude, though, doesn't happen automatically. I said at the beginning of this chapter that it is a choice, and if you choose to have a good attitude, you also have to work at it. Like any goal worth achieving, sporting a positive attitude takes work. You wouldn't expect to run a marathon without practicing, and you won't consistently exhibit a winning attitude unless you cultivate the habit of thinking and acting positively.

Through the hardest of times, I've discovered ten truths about attitude that I share consistently with my audiences. If you pay attention to these truths, you'll grow immensely in solidifying an attitude consistent with your integrity.

1) Good or bad, your attitude goes everywhere you go.

2) The attitude you bring to work every day (and bringing it every single day is crucial!) will dramatically affect your productivity.

3) Nothing colors your personality more than your attitude. Your attitude is how other people will view you.

4) It is a dead-end street to let the things you cannot control interfere with the attitude you can control. You have no control over the weather, interest rates, the economy, the overall industry or profession you work in, or unrest in the Middle East, so letting negative aspects of these things drag down your attitude only sets you up for unnecessary misery.

5) Be loving in the face of injury. The violation and emotional shredding of betrayal is likely the hardest relationship experience to endure and one of the hardest tests for a good attitude. You bless yourself and others, though, if you stay positive even in the face of such a disappointment. Jesus is the greatest example of Someone who loved even those who betrayed Him most cruelly. Learn to love the unloving—unconditionally.

6) Be trusting in the face of disappointment. Give the other person the benefit of the doubt. Everyone needs a second chance. You be the one to give it.

7) Be forgiving in the face of abuse. We all blow it. We all make mistakes. We must be tolerant when facing the shortcomings of others. Forgiveness heals every relationship it touches. The act of forgiving and the state of being forgiven are still very much in vogue.

8) No matter what happened to you yesterday, the way you handle today's circumstances is your choice.

9) If you're a leader, your people will mirror your attitude. Make sure the reflection is one you can be proud of.

10) Winning is an attitude. Legendary football coach Vince Lombardi observed, "There's no greater feeling than to lie on the field of battle totally exhausted but victorious. Conversely, there's no worse feeling than to lie on that same field of battle totally exhausted but defeated." Whichever is your lot, though, a positive attitude will make you an overcomer, ready for the next battle in life (and there will be another battle).

FUELING AN ATTITUDE UPGRADE

If you upgrade your attitude, it will improve the rest of your life in direct proportion to how much you change. Having a good attitude is a catalyst to challenging your mind, encouraging your spirit, strengthening your body, and energizing your will. Mind, body, spirit, and will are interrelated. They're not nurtured and developed separately. When the mind is tested, the will is engaged. When the body excels, the spirit soars. (In the next chapter, we'll talk about this important bodily support for integrity.)

Though decades old, the story of Ben Hogan, a legend on the pro golf tour, remains an unforgettable example of someone whose attitude transformed hopeless circumstances into seemingly superhuman achievement. Hogan's record of winning nine major tournaments—The British Open, The PGA (twice), The U.S. Open (twice) and The Masters (four times!)—is even more stunning when you know "the rest of the story."

Midway through his escalating career, on his way home to Texas from the Phoenix Open, a bus slammed head-on into Ben Hogan's car. The devastating crash left his black Cadillac crushed like a used aluminum can. The doctors who treated Hogan doubted he would survive, much less ever walk again. The golfer suffered multiple profuse internal injuries, a broken foot, smashed pelvis, a broken collar bone, and debilitating damage to his left leg. Yet 14 months after his nearly fatal accident, Hogan limped up the eighteenth fairway at the Marion Golf Club. On the brink of exhaustion and with legs wrapped in ace bandages, he greeted a thundering crowd. Cheers echoed across the Pennsylvania countryside as his final putt added the finishing touch to his victory in the 1950 U.S. Open.

A reporter ran to him and spouted, "Mr. Hogan, how did you make your comeback?" To which Hogan replied, "If I had listened to the 'doomsday people,' I would not be playing in this tournament." Another asked, "What ranks as your top achievement as a pro golfer?" His answer was so simple, it disappointed the journalist: "The thing I'm proudest of is that I got a little bit better every day. My passion for playing golf is what drives me."

Hogan's attitude expressed a thoroughly committed inner life. He showed the integrity of his character by not giving up, a commitment fueled by his passion for golf.

It's easier to have a good attitude if you're passionate about something, so let's focus a bit on passion. I believe that passion, like the attitude it supports, can be cultivated. And it's well worth doing when you consider five amazing things passion can do for you.

1) PASSION DETERMINES YOUR DESTINY.

Study great leaders, and you'll be awestruck by their extreme passion for something: Gandhi for human rights, Sir Winston Churchill for freedom, Dr. Martin Luther King, Jr., for equality, and Bill Gates for technology. Anyone who lives beyond an ordinary life has a great desire for something. Weak desire brings weak results, just as a small fire creates little heat. Michael Jordan, Magic Johnson, and Larry Bird played pro basketball with astounding passion. As a result, they stand among the "greats" of the sports world.

2) PASSION INCREASES YOUR WILLPOWER.

Passion fuels your will. If you want something badly enough, you can find the willpower to achieve it. The only way to have that kind of desire is to develop passion. Fire in your soul keeps you going. An ancient story recounts the experience of a lackluster young man who once approached the celebrated Greek philosopher Socrates to ask for instruction. His casual demeanor betrayed a lack of genuine desire as he presented himself to the great man, "O, great Socrates, I come to you for knowledge." The philosopher responded by leading the young man down to the sea. The two men waded into the water, and Socrates dunked the would-be student underwater. When he let the man up for air, Socrates commanded him to repeat his request. "Knowledge, o great one," he sputtered. The teacher pushed him underwater again, this time a little longer than before. He then repeated the question and received a similar response. Several dunkings later, the philosopher bellowed in the young man's face, "What do you want?" The young man gasped, "Air! Air! All I want is air!" "Good," declared Socrates. "When you want knowledge as badly as you want air, you shall attain it."

3) PASSION ALWAYS REQUIRES YOUR BEST EFFORT.

Dallas Cowboys coach Tom Landry insisted that his players remember a core principle: "Self-respect always demands your maximum effort." When you have passion, it builds your self-respect because you'll see yourself as doing something of value. To keep this truth in mind, say to yourself, "Good is never good enough. I'm going to make excellence my personal standard." Use this thinking to raise the bar on your personal performance in every area of life. You will likely end up attempting (and accomplishing!) some things you've never tried before, but by combining passion and self-respect, you'll go beyond just being successful and become significant in all you do. You'll make a huge difference in your corner of the world.

4) PASSION KEEPS YOU OUT OF YOUR COMFORT ZONE.

NBA coach Pat Riley points out, "Complacency is like a disease sitting on your shoulder, just waiting for you to let your guard down." Don't indulge in musings over how good things were yesterday. In your mind's eye, make last week, last month, and last year look small. Every time the sun comes up and you're blessed with a new day of health, strength, and a sound mind, say to yourself, "I'm going to run a little 'scared and hungry' today. I'm not going to feel complacent or lethargic. I'm not going to be smug or get cozy. I refuse to coast. The only way to coast is downhill, and it doesn't take long to hit rock bottom. I'm going to nurture the vision that sees down the road what most people never see until after they've passed it. I'm going to set the pace, not keep the pace. I'll be the trendsetter." If you keep that foremost and do it, you'll never be out of business in any area of life.

5) PASSION MAKES THE IMPOSSIBLE POSSIBLE.

A fire in your heart energizes everything in your life. That's why passionate leaders are so effective. A leader with great passion and fewer skills will always outperform a leader with greater skills and no passion. Enthusiasm to face new challenges will take you to vistas never before imagined.

SOMEWHERE AFTER THE ATTITUDE

Victor Frankl, author, psychiatrist, and survivor of a Nazi concentration camp, held a high view of attitude: "The last of human freedoms is to choose one's attitude in any given set of circumstances." There's no future in complaining and grumbling about what you don't have. You'll only have a better tomorrow if you first get excited about the things you do have. A thankful spirit replaces anger with love, resentment with happiness, worry with security, fear with faith, wanting to be served with a desire to serve others, jealousy with joy at another's success, and inferiority with dignity.

One spring I was on my way back to Dallas through East Texas, an area well-known for violent thunderstorms. I drove through a torrential mid-afternoon downpour for 30 minutes, and when the storm finally let up, I stopped for gas and to catch my breath from the tense driving. As I leaned back on my car, a spectacular rainbow caught my eye. Every rainbow is caused by the refraction and reflection of the sun's rays in drops of rain and offers seven majestic colors—violet, indigo, blue, green, yellow, orange, and red. Having just negotiated a turbulent storm, I was reminded again that the rainbow is also a long-standing symbol that, regardless of how severe any adversity or crisis, God is still in control. "Hold on, My child," He seems to be saying, "joy comes after the storm." And since the end is joy, there's no reason not to be positive even through the worst of circumstances.

It is this kind of faith and strength that pulled me through three "9/11's" that occurred in my own family.

In 1998, my precious wife Kay was diagnosed with stage 4 ovarian cancer. Since there was no history of cancer in her family and outwardly she was in excellent health, the word from her physician stunned us. Despite 20 months of chemotherapy and some intermittent progress, her situation eventually turned lethal.

During Kay's final months, I took time off from the speaking tour to became her full-time caregiver. She was so weak, I had to bathe, feed, and clothe her. Her inner strength, though, made it a privilege and honor to be there for her. One morning she looked in the mirror and told me she had never looked so ugly, but I responded with all my heart, "Baby Doll, you've never looked more beautiful to me."

"How could you say that?" Kay wondered out loud. "We have a friend whose wife was diagnosed with cancer, and her husband split for a younger woman. Why are you still hanging around for the party?"

"Sweetheart," I told her, "the wedding ring on my finger says I am married to someone very special. It's a commitment from me to you until I draw my last breath." But I was only giving back to her what she had years before offered me. During my dark hours of imprisonment, Kay never wavered in her commitment to me. Joy followed the storm.

A second 9/11: My daughter's bitter divorce included a heart-wrenching custody battle over my granddaughter. The seemingly interminable case sapped us mentally, emotionally, and financially. The reward for our never-give-up attitude, though, was justice in court and a new chance at life for Noelle. Again, joy followed the storm.

My third 9/11: After honorably serving for four years in the United States Air Force in Fairbanks, Alaska, my son Chad returned home devastated. His wife of seven months had walked out on him for another man. Chad succumbed to clinical depression, which severely impaired his judgment. He found himself with the wrong person, at the wrong place, at the wrong time, and lost his freedom to prison-time. Now I caution teenagers and young adults alike to be careful about the friends they keep. The Apostle Paul, too, warns, "Do not be deceived: Bad company corrupts good morals" (1 Corinthians 15:33, NASB). You will become like the friends around you. They will either build you up or tear you down; there is no middle ground. Sharing this warning to help others is the joy after the storm.

These personal 9/11's came upon me at the same time, prompting many friends to ask how I could survive three such calamities simultaneously. My answer: "I'm not surviving, I'm thriving—because God is vital to the equation of everything I am doing. He is the Source of my strength and my staying power." God is the ultimate Source of my attitude.

THE ATTITUDE MAKES THE MAN (OR WOMAN)

More than ten years ago, Virgil Slentz, one of two key mentors for my speaking career, shared with me five valuable principles that solidify the integrity connection between a person's inner character and his or her outer attitude. I still live by them to this day:

1) Always look for new and better ways to serve. Be creative, imaginative, resourceful, and innovative in taking your service to others to a higher level.

2) Become an intense listener; it is a lost art. When you are a real listener, you involve your ears, your heart, and your soul. You also pay attention to what is not being said so you can discern the whole truth about what someone shares.

3) You make a lousy somebody else, but you make a wonderful you. A poor self-image is a weakness you can hide, but it will crack under pressure. Healthy self-esteem, on the other hand, will enhance your ability to think, to learn, to grow, to process information, to manage change, to make right decisions, to solve problems, and to nurture relationships.

4) Take the blame. If you're part of something where blame is being pointed in someone else's direction and you're part of the deal, own up to it. Say to yourself, "I'm healthy enough mentally and emotionally to take all of the blame."

5) Give the credit. If there's credit to be given, don't keep it for yourself. Give all the credit to everyone on the team who helped make the victory possible.

To round out this chapter, I'll summarize the good and the bad you make for yourself, depending on your attitude:

- A sour attitude produces a sour person.
- A resentful attitude produces a resentful person.
- A suspicious attitude produces a suspicious person.
- A positive attitude produces a positive person.

And in case you wonder: Positive is best. Go for it!

LIGHTS...CAMERAS...DISASTER

MY MOTION PICTURE STORY—PART 5

When you're locked up, time drags so slowly the days seem like weeks, and the weeks seem like months, so working two back-to-back eight-hour shifts in the kitchen helped pass the time—a little. But there were two other advantages to my strenuous schedule. One was fresh air. Since smoking was banned in the kitchen, the place was a haven from the haze of cigar and cigarette smoke that choked our living quarters.

Also, working 16 hours a day, six days a week bought me a splendid trade-off. I was the only trusty allowed to watch worship services on television all Sunday morning. That not only helped me keep my sanity but also kept my emotions in check (a single fight could set back a prisoner's parole for a full year). My Sunday "church service" progressed as follows: first, Jimmy Swaggart, then Richard Roberts, "Day of Discovery", Robert Schuller, and finally

Dr. W. A. Criswell. What I soaked in from the sermons, I shared with the inmates and guards during the week. I also wrote key points of the teachings in my diary notes for Kay.

Although the huge turnover in the kitchen crew was an organizational and training challenge (the forced turnover happened because inmates who lost their court cases were transferred to other Texas prisons), I received a remarkable and unexpected culinary education. Many of the top chefs at Dallas' finest hotels had drinking problems and were frequently arrested for drunk driving. Chefs checked in periodically from the Adolphus, the Hilton, the Hyatt, Sheraton, Marriott, and even my old haunt, the Loew's Anatole. They routinely applied for trusty status in the kitchen—and got it, of course. These chefs served as my assistants at the salad bar workbench, and I picked their brains for every morsel of cooking advice they could give. I learned to make a unique salad and garnish it ten different ways. I experimented with their best recipes to concoct things I would never have thought of myself, and after 849 days of incarceration, I walked out of jail with 40 fancy salads committed to memory. (When I came home, Kay and the kids were anxious to sample my delicious food, but I had to say, "I'm sorry. We would need to invite the entire neighborhood. I don't know how to prepare food for just four people." For too long, I had been cooking for 150 officers and 900 inmates for breakfast, lunch, and dinner.)

While I was locked up, I took basketball shooting to a new level. My first "shoot-out" was a command performance. The recreation boss, Mr. Hatley, set me up against an ex-all-state basketball player from Houston who was in jail on drug charges. The champ was 19 years old and itching to whip up on me. The day we squared off, he made 14 free throws before missing. He walked smugly off the court to watch me try. Little did he know that I had shot 99 straight the day before against Coach Hatley, but the boy got lucky. I made just 66 this time around. Only partly daunted, the challenger granted me status as a free-throw marksman but challenged me to a H-O-R-S-E showdown. After five games, he had gotten only one "H" against me. He left shaking his head over what had happened to him.

At least four times a week, I had a chance to go up against one hot shot or another passing through the jailhouse. During my 2.326 years in jail, I never lost a shoot-out to an inmate or a guard, a record that bolstered the respect I had already gained from feeding everyone so well.

One of the miracles I experienced in jail was the chance to have a paying job while incarcerated. Lt. Williams, who was the acting commander for a brief time at the county jail, approached me in the kitchen and warned, "We're about to have a riot in the jailhouse." It seemed that the inmate who was acting as the jail's newspaper delivery man had a bad habit of collecting money in advance for newspapers without writing down the names of subscribers or noting which tank they lived in. As a result, some inmates got papers without paying for them and others who had paid went without. (The U.S. Constitution, by the way, requires that inmates be allowed to buy a newspaper seven days a week if they have the money.)

Lt. Williams explained the situation. "I need an inmate who can run the paper route like a business."

I assured him I would let him know if I thought of someone.

"That won't be necessary," he went on. "Chaffin, you're the new paper man."

"Sir, I don't want to be disrespectful, but that won't be possible. My primary responsibility is to the kitchen, and after a 16-hour day, I'm exhausted."

"Chaffin, let me freshen your memory. The first 30 days you were here, you lost 23 pounds on the regular jailhouse food. Would you like to go back to that?"

Williams wasn't above using a bit of intimidation to get what he wanted, and it worked on me. When I agreed to start the next day, he laid out the rules: each paper would retail for 25 cents, allowing me a ten-cent profit on the morning paper and five cents on the evening. My thoughts flashed back to the paper route I ran with the San Jose Mercury Herald *in California from the time I was 10 until I was 18. I once received a medal from the fire department because on my route one day, I reported a fire which might otherwise have consumed the neighborhood.*

In several days, I had the paper route down to a science. Rather than collect any money in advance, I sold papers on the spot and on each route took a poll as to who wanted one the next day. The guard escorting me was astounded at how smoothly it ran. And I was making $120 a month for the morning paper and $60 a month for the evening paper! At that point for me, $180 was high cotton. Now instead of trying to put money in my account, Kay could take it out each month to go towards car repairs or utility bills.

Entrepreneur that I am, I analyzed my newspaper business and didn't like the fact that I was working harder on the evening paper but only making half as much money as in the morning. I petitioned Lt. Williams to let me add five cents to the list price of the evening paper. All he asked was that I announce the increase to the inmates and guards three days before putting it into effect. The jailhouse population and the guards agreed that my stellar service was well worth the nickel increase, and my profits soared to $240 a month.

The good time didn't last, however. One disgruntled inmate filed a complaint with Capt. Baker, the permanent jailhouse commander, claiming that charging the extra nickel was a violation of his constitutional rights. Capt. Baker demanded a full report from me—both in writing and in person. He called Lt. Williams into his office and in my presence asked, "Chaffin tells me you gave him authorization to raise the Dallas Times Herald *to 30 cents. Is that true?" Lt. Williams denied my claim. I was stunned by such a bold-faced lie! James 1:19 ("Be quick to hear, slow to speak, and slow to anger") was all that kept me from erupting in anger that would have gotten me in a lot of trouble. Even so, Capt. Baker busted me as a trusty and sent me to the 72-hour restriction tank.*

"Of all the trustys in this jailhouse," he chided, "you have been the talk among the officers about how you've turned your life around. What a huge disappointment you are!"

I had no contact with the outside world for 72 hours—no television, no newspaper, no use of the telephone, no visits from my family. One hour into my restriction, guards threw in a prisoner who boasted a double life sentence plus 20 years for capital murder. At 6 feet, 8 inches tall and 300 pounds, he had been brought to Dallas on a bench warrant from a maximum-security prison to testify at an upcoming trial. He paced the floor, shouting obscenities, and claimed he would just as soon kill each of us as to look at us. I sat quietly at a table with my head bowed, but he taunted, "Old man, what do you have to say for yourself?"

"I have no comment," was my only reply. But my mind was racing to assess the situation. Since I had taught hand-to-hand combat as an army drill sergeant, I had a survival strategy in mind in case he attacked. Fortunately, within ten minutes, his four guards scuffled back in to remove the guy, realizing they had made a mistake not to have locked him in solitary confinement.

During my next 24 hours, I wrote a poem called "72-Hour Restriction Is Not a Permanent Affliction," and after my 72-hour impermanent affliction had run its course, I was taken to a cellblock at the Government Center for five days.

Once a prisoner has been busted as a trusty, the chances of being reinstated are practically nil. In my case, though, the guards and officers knew the real story and signed a petition to bring me back to the kitchen. I didn't know it was possible to have a homecoming in jail, but that's exactly what happened when I returned to my regular quarters.

Officers and guards lined both sides of the corridor, cheering, "Chaffin, welcome home!" Some slapped me on the back, thankful that they could "start eating good again." The scene blew me away, and I couldn't hold back the tears. Capt. Baker even called me into his office behind closed doors to acknowledge that Lt. Williams was the one who had lied and that I had been fully vindicated. In addition to returning me to kitchen duty, he offered the paper route to me again, but I declined. One 16-hour-a-day job was enough. And I said good-bye to my $240 a month of riches.

I spent the first half of my incarceration at the Old Jail in Dallas County where Lee Harvey Oswald, accused of assassinating President John F. Kennedy, was killed. My last 14 months were at the Lew Sterrett Justice Center—known as the "Hilton Inn" of jails in America. By jailhouse standards, it was very fancy, and the personnel there also appreciated my talents as a chef. Capt. Toney, the commander, wanted my famous egg salad on the menu every Wednesday. He frequently hosted special guests from around the country and often bragged on my cooking.

One great advantage of the Lew Sterrett Center was the visitation facilities. In the old jail, they had been deplorable. Once I had my personal breakthrough to allow the kids to visit, it sometimes took all of Kay's will to keep coming back. The trusty tank on the seventh floor sat across the hall from the worst tank in the jailhouse. The murderers, rapists, child molesters, and kidnappers housed there shouted obscenities through the air vents all during our visits. The Justice Center, though, offered private visitation booths, which transformed my time with the family. I augmented our visits by sending Kay eight to twelve legal-sized pages of diary notes five days a week. Sometimes she would laugh, sometimes cry, but would always comment, "I can't believe that's going on in there." My writings encouraged her to beef up her prayers for my safety and sanity.

Both the Old County Jail and the Lew Sterrett Center were in downtown Dallas, and neither provided an outdoor campus. Inmates never got to enjoy the sunshine, and that was a hardship. One prisoner transferred to the Old County Jail from San Quentin in San Francisco claimed he would rather serve five years in San Quentin than two years at the Old County Jail—just because San Quentin has an outdoor yard. After 2 years indoors, my skin was so pale, I looked like an albino.

Over time, I realized God had continued in me the work he began during that first dark hour after my sentencing. My values and priorities were being renewed, my attitude improving, and to my surprise, my spirit was brimming with life. I was physically locked up, but I felt more mentally, emotionally, and spiritually free than ever before. God was putting the broken pieces of my life back together—on His terms and in His way.

The one thing I struggled over daily was the financial predicament I put my family in. I beat myself up over why I had been stupid enough to take on Squezze Play in the first place. Through my deep sense of defeat, though, I discovered four steps I would have to work through regarding my massive dose of failure:

1. God could forgive me; my wife and children could forgive me. Others could even forgive me, but if I didn't forgive myself for what I had done, I would never get out of the starting blocks of recovery.

2. I must determine in my heart of hearts never to make the same mistake again and to minimize the magnitude and frequency of future mistakes.

3. It was critical that I learn to attach value to failure as a growth experience.

4. I must reach out to others who are hurting worse than I.

Through jail time, God took me down a road I would never have planned in order to accomplish some things I could never have imagined, but Ecclesiastes 3:11 resonated with my spirit about His purpose: "In My time I will make everything beautiful."

Because Kay's budget was so tight, my brother John sent me $50 a month to finance my basic needs (hygiene items, paper and pens, postage, and other basics I could buy at the jail commissary). The money man brought me $12.50 every Monday morning in the form of Cho-Cho's—U.S. dollars converted into jailhouse paper chits. I made it my goal to have at least $1.00 left over at the end of each week so I could give it to an inmate who seemed especially in need. During the week I would observe someone, for instance, who never got a single visit from a loved one or friends, never received any mail, and never received so much as a dime for his account. It might be a fellow inmate who was a hard worker in the kitchen or a peacemaker in the living quarters. Each time I gave away my dollar, it was an unforgettable joy to see the person's face light up as if Christmas had come. Most were stunned by this simple act of kindness.

Like the visitation facilities, the improvement in overall living conditions at the Lew Sterrett Center was dramatic. The jailhouse population was housed on floors two through nine, and I was one of the first five trustys taken to the second floor. The large cellblock provided eight individual cells with electronic doors that closed at night. The bunks were new—and comfortable!—and each cell had a desk to write on. Every inmate had his own toilet, sink, and shaving mirror, although we still had to share a shower. But it had hot water!

We early arrivers had a stupendous advantage over everyone else. Whenever the population grew at the Justice Center, we were moved upstairs to the next, never-before-inhabited floor. By the time of my parole, I was living on the eighth floor. Somehow, though, it never bothered me that I didn't get to try out the ninth floor.

When you live in a maximum-security setting, risk never takes a day off. Once, a kitchen trusty went berserk, swinging a huge steel paddle at anyone he could hit and screaming that he was innocent, framed by the system. The more everyday risk involved inmates who are inexhaustibly creative in making homemade shanks—crude weapons that can kill or maim.

Although I grew accustomed to the risk from other inmates, one evening I discovered a threat that chilled my soul. I read an article about an inmate in a Texas prison who was the private chef for the warden. When this particular trusty was to be paroled, the warden intercepted the young man's parole papers and locked them in his desk for a year because he didn't want to give up the delicious cooking. Eventually, the trusty was released, discovered what had happened, sued the state, and won his case. But the happy ending didn't make me feel much better. After all, I was still "inside"— and a good cook.

Not long after reading the article, one of the guards fueled my growing paranoia. He joked that since the guards and officers had never "eaten so good," they were putting a permanent "kitchen hold" on me—-meaning I would never be going home.

In spite of my otherwise growing spiritual state, I fell into a deep, clinical depression for three months. I stopped writing diary notes, and when Kay and the kids visited, I said only a few words. And in the kitchen, I ate and ate and ate. When cherry cobbler came out of the oven for the officer's dining room, I helped myself to a king-size portion with a huge scoop of ice cream. Then for dessert after lunch, it would be more cobbler and ice cream. I gained 40 pounds in 90 days, and Satan convinced me I was doomed to spend my life in jail.

The end of my depression began one Sunday morning as I listened to Richard Roberts preach that "God is a God of second chances." "When the hour seems the darkest," he exclaimed, "God is always just in sight." I decided to cling to that hope and reverse my mental and emotional nosedive.

My resolve was bolstered the next day when two U.S. Marshals escorted me to the federal courthouse for the last hearing on the involuntary bankruptcy of Squezze Play. Kay and the children were standing by the courtroom door, and as I passed, Chad called out, "Dad, I've never seen you look so fat!"

I was a sight. I couldn't button my suit pants, so the waist was held together with some wire the guards had given me. My suit coat looked like it was painted onto my torso. I was royally embarrassed.

When I showered that night and pondered my fat belly, I set a goal to lose the 40 pounds before getting out of jail. My game plan: eat 1-1/2 meals a day, no solid food after 6 p.m., and drink lots of water. The day I walked out a free man, I was back down to 200 pounds.

My mental, emotional, and physical turnaround reminded me that regardless of how dismal things seem to be, it's always too soon to quit. As Zig Ziglar–a special friend I'll tell you about in the conclusion of my story–says, "There are no hopeless situations. It's just that some people feel hopeless in some of their situations."

There is nothing sacred about getting knocked down and staying down. The important thing is that when you get knocked down, get back up. The silver lining to any adversity is that the crisis produces turning points in life. As I completed two years of incarceration (with 120 days to go), my heart held a deep and peaceful assurance that upon gaining my freedom, the next chapter in my life would be the most fulfilling ever. I wasn't sure what I would be doing, but I knew God had something extraordinary in store for me.

BILL'S HARD LESSON #5

WHEN YOU'RE BETRAYED AND FALSELY
ACCUSED, RESPOND BY BEING SILENT. THE
TRUTH WILL EVENTUALLY SURFACE, AND
FULL VINDICATION WILL BE THE END RESULT.

Chapter 6

SUSTAINING YOUR INTEGRITY

When I managed the kitchen for the Dallas County Jail, the changes I saw as a result of what I fed the prisoners and guards opened my eyes to a new dimension of living with integrity. I realized that the foods we put in our bodies make a dramatic influence on how well we can express good character and positive attitudes. The saying "you are what you eat" may be only slightly exaggerated. It is certainly true that, physically, you are made of nothing other than what you eat, drink, or breathe, and the way you care for your body—God's temple, according to the Bible—changes your spirit and mind for good or for bad.

Since body, mind, spirit, and will are interrelated, as we've already discussed, a hard look at living with integrity is not complete until we've talked about the way you treat your body. What you do with and for your physical self will make you more or less successful in living with integrity. So let's talk about sustaining your well-being for the sake of your integrity.

THE WELLNESS DREAM

A disciplined and balanced lifestyle triggers wonderful payoffs in the game of life. I've talked about the must-win situations which championship teams and winning people must make happen. Good health is one of those. The foremost reason, of course, is that unless you take care of yourself, you'll simply die, and you're not good for much after that happens. But even before that ultimate consequence, your effectiveness depends on how well you can function physically.

What are you doing to keep your health dream alive? I'm convinced the battle for your life and mine is fought in our blood vessels. If you want to go the distance with your original physical equipment and enjoy optimal health in the process, maintenance is as necessary for your body as for your car. Getting the right rest, eating the right foods, taking the right supplements, and exercising consistently for strength training as well as cardiovascular maintenance protects your most basic wealth: your health.

In my travels I meet people who dream of having or holding on to hope, health, and opportunity. The dictionary defines "hope" as a feeling that what is desired is possible. When you have a strong, healthy body and a sound mind, you help make impossibilities possible. When you strengthen your body, you strengthen your mind and your character. Physical changes produce life changes, and training your body will help you train your mind.

While many people want to feel better, look better, and live better, they don't want to take the time, expend the energy, or spend the money to keep their wellness dream alive. But in physical fitness, you can't fake it till you make it. There are no shortcuts. Dr. Ken Cooper, founder of the Aerobic Center International in Dallas, says there are four things we must do in order to enjoy a high quality of life.

1. Walk three miles a day within 45 minutes, 5 days a week for your cardiovascular system;
2. Strength train;
3. Exercise for muscle tone;
4. Do aerobic routine for endurance.

At age 71, I astound people when I say with all my heart that I believe my most productive years are still ahead of me. That thought alone motivates me to take good care of myself. Fortunately, regular exercise has been part of my lifestyle since I was a teenager. And it only gets more important as I get older. Exercise for people age 70 and up is vital because both men and women in this age group are more susceptible to health problems and physical injuries.

Exercise does more than build muscles and help prevent heart disease. New studies show it also boosts "brain power." Enhanced brain function is crucial to having a strong, active mind, and a clear mind paves the way for everything else.

Many people have an easier-said-than-done attitude toward physical fitness, but I'd like to share with you a revolutionary way to think about staying fit. With one little change in the way you think, you can be on the road to a successful fitness routine.

DEVELOP YOUR OWN BRAG-IMONY

Everybody knows what they should do to stay in shape, right? The biggest problem most people have is that they assume they're doing nothing right, so the road to good health seems impossible to start down. And that's where I'd like to make a difference in your life.

A fellow once observed that sometimes, when he listens to people in church tell about the great things God has done in their lives, it comes across as being more about the people than about God. The "testimony," he noticed, sounds more like a "brag-imony."

It's a funny thought: a brag-imony. Testifying, so to speak, about something you've done. At church, folks should leave their brag-imonies at home, but for keeping yourself physically fit, it is exactly what most people need. Here's why.

To maintain physical fitness you need to be your own coach, and one of the things any coach does for his or her players is to inspire them to make the most of their abilities. A coach picks out what is good and challenges players to excel. If you're going to coach yourself effectively, you've got to do a good job of self-encouragement, and that's where your brag-imony comes in. When your inner voice is speaking, your brag-imony will help you listen only to positive reinforcement.

Figure out what you're doing right—even if it's just one little thing—and tell yourself how great that is. Then take one more little thing you'd like to do, start doing that, and add it to your brag-imony list. I'll give you some ideas about what to put on your brag inventory, but first I'm going to give you my own brag-imony just to show you what one sounds like. When you come up with your own and say it to yourself, you'll also find out just how good a brag-imony can feel.

MY BRAG-IMONY.

I stand 6 feet, 4 inches tall and weigh 200 pounds—of lean muscle mass. Here's how I do it:

1. Six days a week, I walk two to three miles each day (a 15-minute mile);
2. I lift weights four times a week;
3. I do 1,000 tummy crunches daily;
4. I shoot at least 200 shots a day with my basketball;
5. I "eat to live," I don't "live to eat," to borrow some phrases from Benjamin Franklin;
6. I eat lean, modest meals (I never gorge, stuff myself, or otherwise pig out. Although junk food is not part of my diet, once every two weeks, I allow myself a sugary treat.);
7. I drink 70-80 ounces of water every day;
8. I use the finest nutritional food supplements;
9. I get proper rest in order to have the energy I need;
10. I don't use coffee, tea, or any other forms of caffeine. Natural energy gives me all the verve required to accomplish what I need to. I don't count on chemicals to get me going or to get me to sleep. I'm enthusiastic—not depressed—about the realities of life. (Throughout the year I work with teenagers across America in our public and private schools, as well as with kids at risk. I encourage them to say no to drugs, alcohol, and tobacco use of any kind, to get hooked on life, and to get on a natural high. At age 12, I saw how alcohol and cigarettes took their toll on my dad's body, and I was determined to break the cycle of my father's losing behavior. As a result, I've been on a natural high all my life.)

For this balanced and disciplined lifestyle, here's how I've been rewarded:

1. My memory bank stores more than 40 hours of information on 14 different subjects so I can speak without a single note in front of me (that's clarity of thought and sharpness of mind);
2. My resting heart rate is normal;
3. I have strong lung capacity;
4. I enjoy healthy gums and teeth (without a healthy mouth, you're not healthy);
5. My immune system is strong;
6. My blood cholesterol and triglycerides are within normal limits;
7. Physical plumbing works like clockwork;
8. I have tremendous energy (just ask my friends);
9. I handle stress well;
10. My nails and hair are healthy;
11. I have good bone density;
12. My sleep patterns are normal;
13. My fitness helps me avoid back injuries as well as other physical challenges that could slow me down or stop me in my tracks.

When I recount the list of what I do to take care of myself, it makes me feel good. It also inspires me to keep at it. That's why I want you to start your own brag-imony—RIGHT NOW.

Everyone does something good for his or her health. If you think about it for a moment, you will find at least one thing. And that thing is what you need to brag to yourself about, starting immediately. Once you've bragged on yourself a bit, make a list of all the things you'd like to be able to say you're doing, even if you're not doing any of the other things yet (use my list if you want to). Then set this big list aside. If you've only got one thing to brag to yourself about for starters, that's ok. Do you drink lots of water? Tell yourself how good that is. Perhaps you park at the far end of the lot so you have a quarter-mile walk to your office. Good for you! Do you use the stairs instead of the elevator? Bravo! Is the salad bar your favorite lunch? Tell yourself that's great! Do you workout, walk, jog, skip desserts, drink fruit juice instead of soft drinks, avoid caffeine, get to bed on time most nights? Start your bragging rights with whatever it is you do. Give yourself a week to talk nicely to yourself about that one thing. Then pick one more idea from your wish list. Start doing that one, too, and start bragging about it to yourself the very first time you do it. You'll be amazed how good you feel about every tidbit of progress you make. And when your head feels good, it'll make you want your body to keep feeling even better.

AVOID A PERSONAL IMPLOSION

Recently, I saw some video footage of the most spectacular building implosions in history. These remarkable engineering feats require the demolition people to find points in the support structure that must be weakened in order to make the entire building collapse in a heap. The video I watched included high-rise buildings, massive bridges, and soaring communication towers. The thrilling images reminded me that when a person self-destructs, they often implode. Too many people today look good on the outside—nice clothes, great smile, fancy cars—but they are walking time bombs on the inside.

When it comes to health and fitness, the greatest "imploder" around is osteoporosis. Often called a "silent disease," it eats away at your bones, the structural framework of your body. One and a half million people in America suffer bone fractures each year due to osteoporosis. A weak skeletal structure can cause a fracture to the hip, wrist, or spine—even if someone is merely doing normal everyday chores. The debilitation triggered by serious bone breaks include not just physical problems and immobility, but clinical depression and poor self-esteem—serious enemies of integrity.

By age 50, one in every two women and one in four men are diagnosed with osteoporosis. A medical journal recently reported that 10 million people in the United States have low bone mass. Losses due to osteoporosis cost our economy $17 billion a year! The statistics can be discouraging, but you don't have to let them get you down. An easy antidote to add to your brag-imony is walking. Walking gets more muscles and bones involved than any other exercise.

It is incumbent upon adults to be informed, educated, and prepared for the wellness game. Wellness is not all drudgery. It can be a lot of fun. When we challenge the mind, energize the spirit, strengthen the body, and develop the will, awesome things happen!

Three signs hang prominently on the wall of my home gym. One reminds me to "Strive for Personal Best," another claims "I Yearn to Burn," and the third proclaims "Bill Chaffin says, 'Whatever it takes, I will do.'" They are calls to fitness and wellness for youth and adults everywhere. Those who accept this challenge will find new support for living with integrity.

LIGHTS...CAMERAS...DISASTER

MY MOTION PICTURE STORY—CONCLUSION

My fellow inmates warned that when I got my "hat on tight" (that means gaining my freedom), I would never be working with people again because I would have the label of "ex-con." I would have to settle for being a bricklayer, working on a construction crew, laying asphalt, or some other job with lesser people responsibilities. But I'd always loved working with people, and I refused to believe that life was over for me. Their comments motivated me to start exploring what would be next, long before I stepped out into the sun.

My first thought also proved to be my best thought, and I see how God was leading me already. If I wanted to be in the people business, then I should start by contacting one of the best "people persons" on the planet. Zig Ziglar was one of my good friends and a fellow deacon at First Baptist Church of Dallas under Dr. W. A. Criswell. Over an 18-month period while locked up, I wrote Zig nine long letters, each one close to a dozen pages on legal-size paper.

One Sunday afternoon, I called Zig at his home and told him my parole was just around the corner. I asked if he might have a few clients who would consider hiring me when I got out. Evidently he had seen from my letters the tremendous growth taking place in all areas of my life because he immediately suggested that he had four or five possibilities who would be strong candidates to retain my services. He offered to set up interviews for me as soon as my parole was finalized.

A week later, I called Zig to tell him I would be going home in just a few days, and it would be a good time to call his friends on my behalf.

"Bill," Zig replied, "since we last talked, there's been one change." His voice inflection dropped like it fell off the table. My heart sank! I instantly feared that this man with such a strong name, a life above reproach, and a reputation second to none would not risk being identified with me, an ex-con. Maybe the inmates were right after all. Expecting a "worst-case" scenario, I asked softly what the problem was.

"The change is, I want to hire you in the Ziglar Corporation."

I lost it emotionally. His belief in me was a resounding victory I desperately needed. I didn't care what guard or inmate saw tears streaming down my cheeks. After several minutes, I pulled myself together and choked out a reply, "Zig, you will never know what your vote of confidence means to me."

My friend encouraged me to spend ten days with my family and then bring Kay to his office so we could talk about the future. When Kay and I arrived at Zig's office for our meeting, Kay began by thanking Zig profusely for hiring me, but Zig stopped her short.

"Kay, the Ziglar Corporation is not a benevolent organization. If I didn't think Bill was ready for us and we for him, we wouldn't be having this conversation." He let his words sink in and then continued. "I trust Bill is with us a long time so we can be part of his growth and development as a speaker. However, if he steps down and starts his own company someday, we will continue cheering for you all and praying for Bill's success in the future."

Zig's company may not be a "benevolent organization," but I will forever have the highest regard, admiration, respect, and gratitude for how Zig Ziglar used his company to help me. He is authentic Christianity in action. He is a model of integrity, a gentleman–and a gentle man–creative, enthusiastic, life-lover, wife-lover, family man, church man, God's man, and motivator. His confidence in me, his tutelage, and his guidance through the challenges of professional motivational speaking set the stage for my subsequent success in my own motivational business.

It was just two years and four months after that first meeting between Zig, Kay, and me (ironically, about the same length of time I had been in jail) I resigned and formed Turn Key Communications, which later became Bill Chaffin Enterprises, Inc. True to his word (of course), Zig gave me his blessing, and we are good friends to this day.

My darkest hour had begun the process through which God taught me to see all aspects of my life from a radically different perspective. Like putting on glasses, I could see important values clearly as never before. The first of many bright hours of putting my new appreciation of life to work began at 1:58 on the afternoon *of May 25, 1984. I walked out of Lew Sterrett Justice Center to see Kay crossing the parking lot. I broke into a run, swinging two large plastic trash bags as I loped toward my wife. The bags held the treasures from my life of imprisonment—paperback books, a few personal effects, and my remaining diary notes. I dropped the bags, picked up my beautiful wife, and spun her around to celebrate our reunion. Holding her close, I looked up and shouted into the sky I had seen so little of in the previous two years, "So this is freedom!" I knew then I would do everything in my power to never again do something so stupid, so cavalier with my integrity, as to make me lose the precious privilege of liberty.*

BILL'S HARD LESSON #6

SURVIVING YOUR DARK HOUR MEANS YOU HAVE MADE SOMETHING GOOD OF A BAD SITUATION, SO CULTIVATE POSITIVE EXPECTATIONS FOR YOUR FUTURE, AND YOU'LL DISCOVER THAT THE VERY BEST IS YET TO COME.

Chapter 7
PROTECTING YOUR INTEGRITY

Flying home to Dallas from San Francisco, my first-class upgrade landed me a seat next to a distinguished gentleman, sharply appointed down to his manicured fingernails. On an exceptional array of subjects, he proved to be one of the most fascinating conversationalists I've ever encountered. I discovered he was a top executive with a major corporation, and, curious about how he was growing new talent within his organization, I asked, "Who would you consider to be the 'rising super star' in your company?"

"Without a doubt," he quickly responded, "it's a young man who has his MBA from Harvard. He's mature beyond his years. His people skills, communication skills, leadership skills, problem-solving skills, his integrity, and commitment to excellence have him on course to be one of our top executives in the foreseeable future."

He went on to tell me about a significant conversation he had with the young man over lunch six months earlier. The younger executive asked his boss the secret of his success at the company.

"I told him," explained my seatmate, "I've succeeded because of making good decisions!" He chuckled as he recalled the conversation. "'How did you make those good decisions?' he asked me. 'That's a simple one word answer,' I told him, 'Experience.'"

Apparently the younger man still wasn't satisfied because he insisted on asking the boss one more question. "Sir, how did you get the experience?"

"That," the man next to me finally told him, "is a simple two-word answer: Bad decisions!"

I, too, chuckled at this successful man's answer, and I was profoundly impressed with his candor. Here was a man who knew how to grow, how to hold himself accountable for whatever he did—for better or for worse. I also recognized in him a man of sterling integrity because only people who hold themselves accountable can live with thoroughgoing integrity.

ACCOUNTABILITY AND THE FAVOR FACTOR

Introspection and self-examination are keys to healthy living. When you look back to see where you've been, take a fresh look at where you are, but more importantly, to where you could be—in business, family, and your private world. Future possibilities can become exciting. "Sharpening the saw," training, restructuring, doing self-maintenance, learning, changing, and revamping is all part of personal growth.

Life's biggest contest doesn't lie in competing with another company if you're in business. That company's growth target may be too low for you. Neither is the healthiest competition in contending with another person—you may win an individual contest but still fall short of your full potential. Life's most exhilarating challenge is to compete with yourself, to hold *you* accountable for doing the very best you're capable of. When you focus your efforts that way, there's no limit to what you can accomplish. Long-term achievers are rarely the type who "wing it." They keep the bar high for themselves and do the work needed to attain success wherever they intend—at work, family, church, personal growth, athletics. Integrity triggers honesty of purpose, clean sportsmanship, sound principles, and healthy living. Accountability keeps you there.

Your ultimate accountability lies in your relationship to God. Living your life on His terms and doing things His way adds what I call the "favor factor" to your potential for success. When you have favor with God and with man (through a good reputation), you'll live a deeply meaningful life. And when you join forces with others determined to live the same way, you can achieve most anything. Henry Ford claimed of his endeavors that "coming together is a beginning, staying together is progress, but working together is success."

A FINAL CALL

As we wrap up our look at living with integrity, the final "call" I'd like to give you is this call to accountability. Some people cringe at that because they think being accountable to their own standards, to God, and to others threatens their personal freedom. But that is a fool's notion of freedom. A wise person knows that with true freedom comes responsibility. Try to live without responsibility, and your life will be a disaster. Far from being an inhibitor to freedom, accountability protects your freedom by protecting your integrity.

Think carefully about this next statement: Greed and absolute power without accountability corrupt every time. It's a long-standing maxim about what power does to people in any arena of life if there is no accountability. So start with yourself. The next time you make a mistake, mess up, blow it, or experience a major failure, be big enough to own up to the problem you've created. Don't point the finger in someone else's direction or have a "loser's limp" with some phony excuse. Accept 100% of the blame. That's the way to gain experience and keep you on track to making good decisions, as our executive friend explained to his protégé.

Remember, too, that you don't always have to make your own mistakes in order to learn valuable lessons. It is much less painful to learn from someone else's experience than for you to learn a hard lesson on your own. It's been said that anyone can learn from his own mistakes, but the wise man learns from the mistakes of others. If you're wise in this way, you will avoid a great deal of heartache, grief, and pain.

To quote Henry Ford again, he noted, "Even a mistake may turn out to be the one thing necessary to a worthwhile achievement....Failure is the opportunity to more intelligently begin again." When you learn from failure, it is remarkable what new opportunities do, indeed, open up. I'm my own best example of that.

THE OLD MAN AND THE HOOP

Of all the corporate, school, and charity exhibitions I've done, Texas's Bradshaw State Prison was the venue for one of my most memorable basketball shoot-outs. When the prison chaplain told the inmates I was planning a one-of-a-kind basketball demonstration and that I was 62 years old at the time, six of them stayed up all night to make a walking cane for me. They were evidently very gifted at their craft because the cane was a work of art. When I arrived to give my talk, the inmates presented their gift with a good-natured put-down of my abilities. "Basketball Bill," their spokesman intoned, "you're an old popsy with one foot in the grave. You'll be needing this cane to shoot hoops and to just get around."

He thought I was going to respond with some "trash-talking," but all I said was, "Thank you all for the gift. It is something I will treasure. And today, I will let my shooting do the rest of the talking."

That hot July afternoon I was "in the zone," nailing free throws and long shots alike. The inmates couldn't believe their eyes. Most of the time, I hit "nothing but net." It was an immensely satisfying feeling. As always the shooting exhibition set the table for my message, and I gave the inmates two main points to ponder. I wanted them to "awaken the champion within" and "to break the cycle of losing behavior."

I told the guys, "We all have something very much in common…we've all made bad choices. We've all 'blown it.' Every one of us has endured major failures. We have all messed up. Some of us pay a higher price than others. You all are here because of a messed up mind that has led to a messed up life." I offered good advice coupled with hope for a better day.

When I was through speaking, the warden said to me, "I wish every inmate in America could see you shoot hoops and hear your inspirational message. Today you gave the population at Bradshaw State Prison hope to keep on trucking."

The inmates themselves surrounded me after the talk, although they were more intent on pumping me for the secret of shooting hoops so nearly flawlessly. Still, it gave me a chance to drive home my points.

I warned them, "You just can't fake it till you make it. There are no shortcuts. There is no substitute for preparation, regardless of what you do. The way you practice is the way you play. In fact, it takes perfect practice to enjoy perfect play—whether in business or sports." The same is true of living with integrity: Integrity and character take practice.

Finally I made a promise to the inmates that was the hit of the day: "There is no sweat," I said, "when you hit nothing but net. Make every shot a clean shot."

It's possible to hit "nothing but net" in business and in life as well as in basketball, but you've got to start with the right game plan. Aim for what is right and focus on it with everything in you. If I let things distract me while I'm shooting, I lose my focus and concentration. The end result is disappointing and sometimes catastrophic. A lot of people spend a lot of energy working, but their character is so scattered that they never focus on particular goals and outcomes.

If you don't work at improving yourself everyday, you will be stuck in the same place, doing the same thing, hoping the same hopes, and never gaining any new ground. Integrity uplifts your mental, emotional, spiritual, relational, financial, physical, and professional well-being.

So: practice, practice, practice living with integrity every day. It's the only way to a life of Nothing but Net.

Epilogue
LIFE MUST GO ON

There is no future in looking back,
Agonizing over what might have been.

I am seizing the moment and pursuing my dreams,
Praising God that my faith and hope is in Him.

To climb any mountain that stands before you,
Requires determination, inner strength, and grit.

Don't panic when unexpected surprises
    show up on this journey of life,
God somehow makes everything fit.

When you learn to live in the present,
Accepting life's challenges, trials and struggles
That sometimes don't seem so fair,

God will always help you pick up the pieces,
And rebuild your life
For it's your burdens that He wants to bear.

Let's review what it takes to begin again,
And you must rank attitude at the top of the chart.

Remember one thing:
Whenever a "9/11" or "personal tsunami" hits you,
God is still in the business of healing a broken heart.